# Good
# Enough
# *Is Never*
# Good
# Enough

# Good
# Enough
# *Is Never*
# Good
# Enough

## *A Personal Prescription For Management*

## KEVIN WELDON

📚 Angus&Robertson
An imprint of HarperCollins*Publishers*

# Acknowledgements

The author wishes to acknowledge Phil Mathews, who edited and helped me with his great professionalism, and my daughter, Leonie, who trapped me into starting this book as notes to help her in business.

**Angus&Robertson**
An imprint of HarperCollins*Publishers*, Australia

First published in Australia in 1995
Reprinted in 1995

Copyright © Kevin Weldon 1995

**HarperCollins*Publishers***
25 Ryde Road, Pymble, Sydney, NSW 2073, Australia
31 View Road, Glenfield, Auckland 10, New Zealand
77-85 Fulham Palace Road, London W6 8JB, United Kingdom
Hazelton Lanes, 55 Avenue Road, Suite 2900, Toronto, Ontario M5R 3L2
*and* 1995 Markham Road, Scarborough, Ontario M1B 5M8, Canada
10 East 53rd Street, New York NY 10032, USA

National Library of Australia Cataloguing-in-Publication data:

Weldon, Kevin, 1933– .
   Good enough is never good enough:
   a personal prescription for management.
   ISBN 0 207 18727 4.
   1. Management. 2. Management—Australia. I. Title.
658.

Edited by Ian Cockerill.
Cover photograph by Stuart Spence.
Printed in Australia by McPherson's Printing Group.

10 9 8 7 6 5 4 3 2
99 98 97 96 95

# CONTENTS

# KEVIN WELDON:
# A BRIEF BIOGRAPHY

- Commissioned Lieutenant in the RAN (Reserve) in 1956.
- Remained involved in surf lifesaving movement, holding many posts. Now member of President's Board of National Council of Surf Lifesaving Association of Australia.
- Foundation president of World Lifesaving, which brought water-safety organisation throughout the world under one umbrella.
- Founded Earthwatch, a voluntary organisation that supports scientific expeditions.
- Served on variety of committees and boards, notably Powerhouse Museum (Sydney), Institute of Aboriginal Studies (Canberra).
- Has a long association with Bali. Introduced surf lifesaving to the island and has an important collection of local art.
- Established Gwinganna on the Gold Coast hinterland as a study centre.
- Best-known hobby is collecting Tiger Moth and amphibian aircraft. He flies regularly, competing and touring in Australia and overseas.
- Member of the Cruising Yacht Club of Australia and Royal Prince Alfred Y.C. Kevin Weldon is married with three children.

## 1960s

- As founding managing director of the Paul Hamlyn Group in Australia, publishes a string of best-sellers with vigorous marketing. Launches successful *Australia's Heritage* partworks.

- Successfully launches Music for Pleasure, Australia's first budget record company.

## 1970s

- Continues to build best-selling list in Australia and develops local publishing lists in New Zealand and the Philippines. Launches further successful partworks: *Australia's Wildlife Heritage, New Zealand's Heritage, New Zealand's Wildlife Heritage* and the *Filipino Heritage.*
- Launches *Geo*, Australia's first national geographic magazine.
- Acquires Australian publishers Lansdowne Press (Melbourne), Ure Smith (Sydney) and Jacaranda (Brisbane).
- Enters a joint venture with Hanna Barbera, US animation film producers; develops the first large animation studio in Australia.
- Creates a number of best-sellers with a landmark marketing strategy, promoting books on television and in conjunction with major newspapers.
- Develops a prestigious limited edition list, specialising in nature and art.
- Starts significant library of rare Australian books and an Australian art collection.
- Acquires Rigby Ltd (Adelaide), general and educational publishers.
- Resigns from Paul Hamlyn 1979.

## 1980s

- Guides takeover of British publisher Marshall Cavendish by *Straits Times*, Singapore. Briefly chairman of Marshall Cavendish to steer it to record profit of £6 million the following year.
- Forms Kevin Weldon & Associates and launches a successful publishing list. *Day in the Life of Australia* an instant best-seller.

- Enters local US market with joint ventures, notably in Texas.
- Founds Earthwatch in Australia, a voluntary body to fund scientific expeditions.
- Publishes *The Macquarie Dictionary*, a definitive work that is now the undisputed arbiter of the Australian language.
- Joint venture with major newspaper groups John Fairfax Ltd (Sydney) and David Syme Ltd (Melbourne) for a major bicentennial work, *Australians: a historical library*.
- In 1985 purchases 50 per cent of the Paul Hamlyn Group (Australia) with James Hardie Industries Ltd. Purchases the balance three years later. Retail sales increase by about $10 million a year. Name changed to Weldon International.
- Takes an interest in films, developing complementary book products including *Wall of Iron* and *Over China*.
- Initiates policy of devolution in which Weldon International is formed into relatively small, creative publishing and marketing units, which operate independently with a responsibility for profitability to a small executive centre. No territorial limits imposed on any of the companies, to encourage export.
- Starts vigorous offshore drive that results in Weldon International exports accounting for 55 per cent of Australia's total export of book product.
- Opens offices in US and UK to develop local publishing and marketing.

## 1990s

- The group's policy of devolution delivers growth, particularly in offshore activity. Weldon International rises to 183rd of Australia's top 500 exporters.
- Publishing companies of Weldon Inter-national are now firmly established in the US and UK. The Weldon policy of devolution continues as spin-off publishing activity warrants.
- Local and US educational publishing for elementary schools becomes so successful that it is reorganised for marketing

overseas through jointly-owned marketing companies in US and UK. Mimosa is also active in Canada, New Zealand, Southeast Asia and South Africa.

- Produces national commemorative books for governments in Singapore, China, US and Indonesia.
- Establishes Gwinganna in the Gold Coast hinterland for study groups.
- Becomes founding president of recently formed International Lifesaving Federation, which is an amalgamation of the worlds three largest water-safety organisations. The Federation has over sixty member countries and over 25 million members.
- Receives Order of Australia for his service to the publishing industry and to water safety.
- Retail turnover of Weldon International exceeds $160 million.

# Weldon International

The Weldon International Group of Companies is proud to be the largest independently owned publisher in Australia. We have achieved this position by building a solid core business in Australia and then expanding our horizons to major world markets. We now export 60 per cent of our titles, which accounts for two thirds of all Australian book exports. Proudly Australian, Weldon International has acquired a position in the list of the top 250 exporters.

## Weldon International Group of Entities

### Consumer Book Publishing
Weldon Owen Pty Ltd
      Weldon Reference Inc. (USA)
      World Living Art Pty
      Weldon Owen Inc (USA) — 50 per cent
Weldon Russell Pty Ltd
Weldon Kids Pty Ltd
Harlaxton Publishing Ltd (UK)
Weldon Information Enterprises Pty Ltd

### Educational Publishing
Mimosa Publication Pty Ltd
      Kingscourt Publishing Ltd (UK) — 60 per cent
      Mimosa Marketing (US) — 50 per cent

### Direct Distribution
Beaut Books Australia Pty Ltd
Social Club Books Pty Ltd — 49 per cent
The Family Book Co Pty Ltd

# INTRODUCTION

*Good Enough Is Never Good Enough* was chosen as this book's title because it is a phrase I have often used to stimulate, to drive, and to monitor my own efforts. It encapsulates an attitude that I believe would be wonderful to embrace as a national outlook, encouraging us all to lift our game to produce ever higher standards of goods and services. It need not be confined to business. It can be applied to any endeavour, whether health care, essential services, transport or roads. In short, everything we do.

I believe that many Australians share my frustration with substandard quality, wherever it surfaces. It deeply concerns me when it is the result of inadequate effort by my fellow workers or by others such as traders, merchants, bureaucrats, accountants, bankers, doctors, politicians and journalists. A "good enough" attitude is like an insidious moth eating at the fabric of our commerce and services. If ignored, it will undermine our future and cost us the marvellous quality of life we take for granted.

Too many people with the power to influence accept far less at present in the short-sighted belief that they can get away with a slack performance or a shoddy product. This abrogation of the responsibilities of leadership is the root of the problem, yet my business peers continually blame the workers! The facts, however, show that while most workers were sacrificing a great deal in the last decade, it was largely incompetent boards and weak management that precipitated the collapse of hundreds of large companies. Greed was not the sole cause of this travesty. A sloppy "good enough" mentality created poor standards of financial control, poor people motivation and questionable business morality.

Though I am near the end of my business career I still feel bound to strive for better standards because I believe they can make Australia a better place in which to live. If this means telling people their product or service is of a second-rate quality, so be it. At least it is with the best of intentions. Our future depends on it.

Some time ago my children asked me to put down some of my business ideas and philosophies. This book is the result. It does not pretend to be the definitive treatise on business management. Instead, it is a collection of the ideas and experiences that have helped me. I trust that parts will be similarly helpful to a wide range of readers, whether business people, workers or students.

If this book can persuade readers that "good enough is never good enough" then it will have been well worth the effort.

KEVIN WELDON

# CHAPTER I

# BUILDING A WINNING TEAM

Controlling men is like handling a piece of string. If you push it,
it will go anywhere. If you lead it, you can make it
go anywhere you want.

GENERAL D. EISENHOWER

Morale, according to General Patton, is an attitude that enables
your troops to do the thing they most hate — and love doing it. He
was right. Morale is the most important asset of a good team, but it
doesn't just happen. It must be cultivated by astute leadership.

The first task is to create a flexible environment. Any group will
have in its ranks a spectrum of physical attributes, educational
qualifications and aptitudes. The working environment must be
flexible enough to first identify each individual's strengths and then
offer sufficient freedom for them to flourish.

A leader must also be aware of any limitations in the team and
use the collective talents available to shore these up. Make no
mistake, everyone has weaknesses. These must be accommodated
rather than highlighted. They should never be ignored. If we want
one of the team to design the greatest, most splendidly innovative
product for us, we must give them enough latitude to exploit and
develop their creativity. That need not mean, however, that we
should assume that their costings will be as impeccable as their
design talent.

I once had an amazing salesman who could obtain seemingly
impossible orders. But he was always behind with his daily sales
reports. Paperwork was clearly not his strong suit, but in this case I
asked the sales manager not to hassle him. "Just check the massive
volume of invoices coming through daily from his territory," I
cautioned. As a result we enjoyed the best fruits of his talents, which

far exceeded any clerical shortcomings. And we were not the only ones to profit from this attitude. This man is now a multi-millionaire and owner of one of the largest music companies in Australia.

## LEADERSHIP

"Controlling men is like handling a piece of string. If you push it, it will go anywhere. If you lead it, you can make it go anywhere you want." General Eisenhower may have been talking of his troops, but his observation applies equally to business, the suburban football team and the local fire brigade.

In business, team leaders must lead by example. They must work longer hours and pursue the company's objectives with vigour and enthusiasm. For a team to respond positively, leaders must also have humility and a genuine love for their fellow man. And although fair at all times, they must also be capable of making the hardest decisions (after careful consideration). In short, they must treat their team members as they would like to be treated themselves. When appropriate, they should also relax and give themselves and their team a period when they run a little loose. Sit down and enjoy a few drinks. Allow the team to get frustrations (and they will have some) off their chests. And if the leader is smart enough to listen, there will be many times when a member of the team will, perhaps unwittingly, identify a hole in the company's fence that can be quickly repaired before too much damage is done.

If a leader is to build a good team they must first be themselves. Certainly most of the great achievers and leaders I have met had distinctly different personalities. Never try to model yourself on what you think a leader should look like or how one should behave. I have seen many fail in leadership because the true individual never emerged. They squandered their energy playing a perceived role.

If the leader has the authority to set the objectives and strategies of the team, he or she must do so in very simple terms. Too often team members are given reams of instructions and figures that leave them totally confused. For example, if the objective is to obtain export orders, then this must be translated into a target of "X" amount of sales. The strategy might be to produce a top quality product at the lowest possible price to achieve these sales.

*When I was with the Hamlyn Group, concerts were occasionally performed in the warehouse as a diversion for busy staff.*

Once this is established, the leader should continually remind the team of this simple, unambiguous challenge. It does not need to be couched in 100-page company manuals.

Similarly, a leader must constantly strive to keep the team environment buoyant, encouraging the team to use its ability to tackle the most difficult tasks. This can require a bit of grit, because business is not without risk, and the boldest targets are often the riskiest. Team members who attack their job boldly may, in their enthusiasm, expose themselves and their leader. There will inevitably be setbacks, even failures. But a good leader must have the starch to allow an individual of the team to fail. I once heard success described as "a failure is a failure is a failure is success". There is always a price but, handled properly, enthusiasm and initiative are infinitely more rewarding than the efforts of timid staff who so dread the consequences of failure that they shun responsibility and commitment. This doesn't mean that a team member who makes a cock-up should be spared a blast. But it is important for team spirit that, when someone does makes a terrible mistake, they are encouraged to promptly admit, "I stuffed it up". Once it is exposed, you can clear the problem and get on with the job.

Team members should never feel so threatened by dismissal that silence seems their only option. Some of my great failures (and there have been a few) might have been avoided if a team member had not hidden a mistake because they were too terrified to admit it. If they'd had the confidence to admit their mistake we might well have chosen a different course of action. At the very least we might have salvaged more by battening the hatches earlier.

## Integrity

There can be no compromise of honesty and integrity in business if you want to achieve self-respect and the respect of the wider community. This must emanate from the team leader, who must rigorously ensure that everyone in the team follows suit. "My word is my bond" might have an old-fashioned ring to it, but it remains as valid today as ever. Perhaps more so, because of the pace and complexity of modern business.

You show me a business in which the leadership's honesty has been compromised and I'll show you a business without spirit.

## Control

"We must control this mob." How often have you heard this, whether it relates to a group in a classroom, a company division, or a football club? I don't even like the word "control", because every time I hear it said it is delivered with a superior air or combative attitude.

I get particularly put off when it is used by people with less talent than those they are controlling. What we should really be aiming for is to provide people with freedom within boundaries and the guidance to achieve their objectives.

Checking the progress towards their objective is the best and only control that is effective. And it must be done regularly. Don't

wait until it is too late because you have been too lazy to check.
One of my assistants once said of control:

> It's like holding a small bird in the palm of your hand. If you hold it
> too tight, you will crush it and destroy it. If you hold it too loosely, it
> will fly away. If you hold it just right, you will achieve all you want.

A leader must have the ability to hold their team like a bird. Just right.

# FINANCIAL CONTROL OR STRANGULATION?

There's only one thing worse than losing money — that's thinking you're making money when you're in fact losing it!

SIMON GOMPERTZ

I had an absolutely brilliant financial controller who once lamented, "Everyone hates accountants. We are human and, like everyone else, love to be loved — at least *some* of the time!"

We often hear business failures blamed on the accountant or their influence over the chief executive. Yet most failures at this level of business relationships come about because:

- The chief executive bullies the financial controller into submission while spurning his or her advice.
- The financial controller's recommendations on the value of assets are ignored by the board.
- The financial controller's cautionary forecast regarding the cash flow is ignored because the chief executive does not believe an accountant capable of really understanding the business.
- The chief executive forfeits leadership by allowing the accountant to make decisions instead of using the advice as an aid to management decisions.

To avoid these pitfalls you need a very strong figure-person running in tandem with a tough chief executive. The accountant should write a prescription for his or her chief, but only the chief should decide whether to take the medicine. The chief may well die, whether the medicine is taken or not, but the decision must be the chief's, not the accountant's.

Having said that, *sound financial control* is absolutely essential in business. These are some of the first steps I would take.

## CHART OF ACCOUNTS

Set up a numbering system and description for every item that appears on the profit and loss account, balance sheet and cash flow chart. This is particularly important for a group of companies, whether local or international. Its purpose is to ensure that all financial, marketing and management people speak precisely the same language — a prerequisite for proper accounting and financial reporting.

Many problems in financial reporting arise because various divisions wrongly assume that *their* definitions are the same as those of other divisions. Unless the definitions are set out clearly in a chart of accounts, and followed by all divisions, efficient financial reporting is impossible.

## MONTHLY MANAGEMENT AND FINANCIAL REPORTING

Every company, no matter how big or small, must put out a monthly profit-and-loss balance sheet and updated cash flow as soon after the end of the preceding month as possible. It should be completed no later than the end of the first week of the new month. I am told, however, that the end of the second week of the new month is a reasonable average.

## FINANCIAL MANAGEMENT

Financial managers must stand their ground, keep impeccable accounts and never allow themselves to be bullied into changing the facts. They can always sue for millions if they are dismissed for their honesty!

They must always update the cash flow, because a report without a meaningful cash flow is useless. My old friend and financial adviser, Simon Gompertz, used to say, "There's only one thing worse than losing money, that's thinking you're making money when you're in fact losing it!"

This has happened to me and I have seen it happen in other companies. I believe I could quickly prove that a lot of businesses out there that confidently report profits are actually losing money. The 1990s are strewn with the wreckage of such companies from the 1980s.

## Valuation of Assets

The correct valuation of assets is one of the most critical functions of a financial manager. Many companies value their assets on an annual basis, but today's world moves very fast, particularly the fluctuation of currencies. It is imperative that the monthly balance sheet reflects the true value of assets *as determined that month*. The consolation for such discipline is obviation of the need for a huge revaluation of assets at year end.

Whatever policy is laid down must remain consistent from one year to the next and not be altered at the whim of the chief executive or board. The net assets as described in the balance sheet must reflect a true and correct value. It is the only real protection a shareholder has; after all, the figure virtually expresses the true value of shareholders' funds.

Most companies go under because of bad debts and over-investment in inventories. From my experience, most companies like to think they value their inventories by the LIFO or FIFO method (Last In First Out or First In First Out). In reality they tend to value by what I call the LIVER method, which depends entirely upon the state of the manager's liver at the time. How often do managers claim, when stock is moving slowly, that they will sell it next year? Perhaps they will, though they are more likely to be kidding themselves. Managers are painfully reluctant to wear a writedown for stock provision, because it reflects on their performance.

The only correct method for proper financial valuation is the Ageing Method. This is based solely on the number of months' stock in hand, as indicated by the sales rate. It quickly determines whether you have one month's or five years' stock. Here again, this has to relate back to gross profit margins. If you have several years' stock of an item with a low gross profit rate, you aren't going to make it! But the Ageing Method will, if reviewed monthly, prevent over-valuing this asset.

A similar formula should be applied to work in progress. How often do you find work in progress started on a project that is subsequently suspended for months or even years, yet the original investment still appears in the balance sheet as an asset of work in progress at that date?

Like stock, it should be written down by an Ageing Method. For every month that there is no expenditure on a work-in-progress item, a provision should be made to write it off. This has two dramatic effects. The people concerned get off their backsides and admit the project will never be finished, or they spend more money and complete it. Furthermore, this asset will be conservatively valued in the balance sheet.

## PRESENTATION OF THE MONTHLY PROFIT AND LOSS AND BALANCE SHEET

Many people in management don't really understand the monthly profit and loss and balance sheet, but somehow bluff their way through. This is partly because reports are nearly always presented to suit the accounting department rather than management. I always insist that these figures be presented in a simple form so that they are readily understood by less numerate minds. This is always hard to accomplish because, like all specialists, accountants love to present their work in a form and language that only other accountants understand. I do not suggest that their specialist role is unnecessary, but reports for management must be abbreviated and simplified for more effective comprehension. Here are some of the elements I insist upon in the monthly reports:

- Details of every item that makes up the total operating overhead.
- Gross sales
  Less returns
  Net sales
  Gross margin
  Provisions
  Gross profit
- All figures must be horizontally and vertically totalled.

- Ratios must be put down beside all items in the Profit and Loss columns and vertically totalled.
- Ratios must be put down beside all items in the Profit and Loss Account, starting with gross sales as 100 per cent and the other items as a percentage of this figure.
- The report should show a comparison with the original forecast and/or revised forecast, year to date, and same period last year.

## FUNDS EMPLOYED OR NET ASSETS

I believe funds employed and net assets are the two items (some companies use one or the other) which are the real measure of performance, that is, the net profit as a percentage of total funds employed or net assets employed.

## THE THREE MONTH ADVANCE ROLL OVER CASH FLOW FORECAST

Companies that don't forecast three months ahead each month in order to anticipate any major change in cash requirements are likely to run into serious trouble. They find themselves with no money in the bank and no time to act. This is a difficult piece of reporting to introduce. Everyone wants to dodge the hard work needed to prepare it, and in the early days of introduction it's not always accurate. After months of perseverance, however, it is a wonderful tool for cash management.

## MANAGER'S REPORT

This should be brief — no more than two pages — but should have enough information for other managers or boards to identify trends, shortfalls, highlights and major problem areas. The report should be divided into quantifiable and non-quantifiable sections.

In order to give meaning to variations and deviations, it is necessary to compare the present results with the figures that were budgeted when the cash resources were allocated.

This is not to say that everything was known when the original budget was prepared and that an absolute standard was set in concrete. What is known, however, is the intended cash/debt position — the cash earmarked to finance the business. By attempting to adhere to that financial commitment, material variations can be highlighted so that a revision to the budget can be started. This will ensure that the original cash commitment is not exceeded, unless otherwise agreed by the board or the owners.

In that regard, therefore, the profit/loss and net funds absorbed become the key figures on which to report. There is no need to report on each sub-line other than to show the figures and highlight the major varying component.

**To date — actual profit/loss versus budget profit/loss**

|                                | ACTUAL | BUDGET | VARIANCE |
|--------------------------------|--------|--------|----------|
| Net sales                      |        |        |          |
| Gross profit %                 |        |        |          |
| Gross profit                   |        |        |          |
| Expense (other than interest)  |        |        |          |
| Interest                       |        |        |          |
| Net                            |        |        |          |

To summarise, the following elements must be adhered to by both financial management and general management if the company is to succeed:

- Prompt management accounts. For instance, a profit and loss balance sheet should be released as soon after the end of the month as possible.
- All assets must be valued monthly and proper provisions made monthly. Never change the method of valuing the assets or reporting from one year to the next just to suit management or board results.

**Net funds — actual date versus same date in budget**

| | ACTUAL | BUDGET | VARIANCE |
|---|---|---|---|
| Prepayments/Deferred costs | | | |
| Work in progress | | | |
| Stock | | | |
| Receivables (other than inter-divisional balances) | | | |
| Investments | | | |
| Intangible assets | | | |
| Fixed assets | | | |
| Payables (other than debt and interdivisional balances) | | | |
| Accruals | | | |
| Deferred income | | | |
| Net | | | |
| Non-quantifiable factors | | | |
| New developments / Major problems | | | |

# THE FIVE-YEAR PLAN

Producing a company five-year plan every year is a real challenge. It is more like gazing into a crystal ball than precise forecasting, but business predictions must be made and quantified. (I believe three years is a better time span because the calculated guesswork is that much better, although it is the thinking process that matters more than the accuracy.)

I have found that the real benefit of preparing a five-year plan is setting benchmarks for major decisions such as targeted acquisitions, mergers and divestments and, more importantly, estimating the funding required to enact the plan. Yet, for all this planning, experience teaches me that dramatic growth and success spring as much from random opportunities as from the merits of any five-year plans. The best circumstance, of course, is when a random opportunity is in accord with a five-year plan.

I recall an example of this in the mid-1970s when the James Hardie Group became painfully aware that most of their profit came from a building board based on asbestos, a material rapidly losing favour.

They decided they had to make a large acquisition that would give them enough time and earnings to develop a replacement material. With all the planning in place they were poised, waiting. One of the top 100 publicly-listed companies at the time was Reed Consolidated Industries, owned 75 per cent by Reed International (London) with a 25 per cent Australian shareholding. When Reed International decided to embark on a divestment program of all their Australian, South African and Canadian companies, Hardie's advisers saw their opportunity and made a quick offer of $60 million for the 75 per cent shareholding. It was the largest corporate takeover in Australian industry history and gave Hardie's just the impetus they needed to successfully negotiate a testing period in their development.

Many opportunities such as this will arise for those who are properly prepared. Consider the exciting, privately-owned company that seems impregnable to acquisition. Suddenly, the owner dies and the remaining family has no interest in becoming more involved in the company. A quick offer can be successful.

Planning, it must be admitted, has little bearing on the seizing of other opportunities. Years ago I worked in London with a fellow who was a director of Lord Thomson's family company. Thomson was then owner of the London newspaper, *The Times*, and the Hudson Bay Trading Co., among others. The company had just become involved with North Sea oil and their profits jumped in one year from £7 million to £27 million. I remember commenting to the director what an unusual diversification it was to go from the businesses they were in to the development of North Sea oil wells. "It must have been good planning," I ventured.

Planning had little do with it, he explained. The son of Lord Thomson had been at university in England with one of the Middle Eastern oil sheiks who, on a later visit to London, had suggested the young Thomson place some "seed" money with him because he thought North Sea oil would be successful.

Lord Thomson agreed to put up £1.3 million for the first stage. The real development came later, with the investment of £13 million. Lord Thomson then decided that, because of the size of the investment, he should hand it over to his publicly-listed Thomson Group. This he did with great success. So much for grand corporate plans: just two friends from university renewing a friendship. It is not an isolated story, either.

In the 1970s, Rupert Murdoch moved swiftly to acquire almost 50 per cent of Australia's largest domestic airline, Ansett. As Murdoch was primarily in publishing, all the young MBAs around the city were agog at the brilliant planning that must have been behind such a lightning fast move at the right moment. I happen to know that Rupert Murdoch was playing tennis in Sydney at the time a big parcel of Ansett shares became available. A stockbroker called from Melbourne to ask if he was interested. After a few moments consideration he decided to buy and in a very short time he owned 50 per cent of Ansett with TNT. The deal was the result of Murdoch's instinctive genius for a good deal and an impeccable sense of timing. Planning had absolutely nothing to do with it.

There is, of course, more than one way to skin a cat and, I am told, the New Zealander Sir Ron Brierley represents the opposite approach. This brilliant corporate takeover expert spends a great deal of time on detailed planning, studying every aspect of the target company before making his move. To we outsiders he always appeared to move so suddenly that it seemed he was operating on a whim or some sharp instinct. However, it was quite the contrary.

(As a general rule, I've found that when acquisitions are made without enough planning, the price paid is usually too high — though over a longer term the higher price may prove to be a bargain.)

In summary, the ideal blend would seem to be a combination of long-term planning, instinctive timing and an ear for good advice.

# CHAPTER 3

# PAPERWORK OR PAPER CHASE?

> During my thirty-odd years in business, I have seen
> paperwork increase in direct proportion to the very
> technology that was supposed to reduce it.
>
> K.E.W.

I have met perhaps ten business people whom I regard as incredible successes. Their success, by my measure, is the ability to run a business profitably over many years with an extremely good return on funds, or the tenacity to build an extremely large corporation from scratch. Above all, they make lots of money!

One attitude they all share is a loathing of pointless paperwork. They have throttled it in their organisations. They refuse to accept report summaries that exceed one page, and they have minimised internal and inter-company memos. What they do insist on, however, is a weekly summary of profitability and cash flow, no matter where they may be in the world.

## THE EVOLUTION OF PAPERWORK

During my thirty-odd years in business, I have seen paperwork increase in direct proportion to the very technology that was supposed to reduce it. Some of us can remember the big breakthrough that came with carbonless paper. Then followed — what excitement! — the electric typewriter. And now, the word processor. All spewing out more words, but less communication. In between came the technological leap that undoubtedly created the tallest piles of useless paperwork, the portable tape recorder. It enabled managers to dictate reports, memos and letters whether travelling in cars or planes or just relaxing at home ... then toss the tapes to their secretary to type. And what unedited garbage it produced! One could always identify such letters by their interminable length.

## THE "F" MACHINE

There are, nevertheless, some technologies which deliver on their promise. Among those at the top of my list is the fax machine. I well recall how impressed I was when the fax was developed. I suggested that we install one immediately in all branch offices. The management group with which I was involved hesitated, and, predictably, warned me to first test the technology. (Why do people need to test technology that is so obviously useful?) I ploughed ahead anyway and had faxes installed in all production areas and branch offices under my control. Today I wonder how business functioned before the fax.

## BAD HABITS

However, like every communication aid, it can breed bad habits. If management is not careful, all supervising levels will fax information for decision-making to the next level instead of making the decision themselves. This will continue all the way up to the chief executive, who will end up buried under hundreds of pages of faxed information that should never have reached his desk.

Faxes are extremely helpful when travelling, but every manager knows that an irritating proportion of the daily pile of faxes — scanned over breakfast — carry utterly useless information.

As with all other paperwork, instructions should be concise and clear. There should be an extraordinarily strong reason to send a fax, either internally or externally, when a phone call would do the job. If a fax is needed it should be brief, in the manner of a telex message or telegram.

## THE WRITTEN REPORT

Those of us who have spent time as directors of public companies will appreciate the frustration of writing a board paper to apply for capital outlay for a building, a plant, machinery, or an acquisition. The board would invariably find the paper too complex and ask for it to be abbreviated. As soon as it was condensed, the board would complain there was insufficient information!

This happened to me on several occasions. After one such stream of unsuccessful submissions, my financial director exploded with frustration, "When the bloody board knows what they want, we can give it to them. Until they know what they want, we can't!"

For reasonably-sized public companies, every subsidiary or division is required to produce that dreaded document, the annual business plan. It is usually a huge document, showing full projected profit and loss with detailed sales forecasts, and a breakdown of all operating overheads with, of course, impeccable cash flows.

Included with the figure work is the voluminous written report which explains, with the most elaborate fiction, how an astonishing 10 per cent increase in all revenues will be achieved in spite of the division having failed to achieve the previous year's plan.

I worked with a large group several years back which had some 100 subsidiary companies. The Australian group, in turn, was a subsidiary of a large international group. All told, there were 2500 subsidiary companies plodding away, churning out these reports around the world.

The reports were all sent to the local chief executive, who had them summarised and dispatched to the poor chief executive in London. There is absolutely no way that either chief could possibly have read all of them in the time available.

The real benefit of producing these reports (if properly organised) is that the business is examined in great depth annually and the sales forecast produced on a known segmentation and a projected sales base. This sales forecast is a key element and considerable time should be spent on this projection — though not, as most people do, by plucking figures out of the air that are vaguely similar to last year's. On the other hand, operating overheads need relatively little study to arrive at what next year's costs should be.

The most successful plans I've had submitted to me from divisions were those which expressed sales I knew were achievable.

**"Guess where we're hanging out now?"**

*A favourite change-of-address card.*

These forecasted lower sales than the previous year, but kept the operating overhead to sales percentage at the targeted ratio. This ensured no blow-out in costs. If opportunistic sales occurred on this low operating level, then very rewarding profits would inevitably follow.

## STATIONERY

### Letterheads

Whether a letterhead is exquisitely designed, coloured, embossed and gilt-edged, black-and-white or just plain, is not going to make much difference to the success or failure of a company — particularly when most communication these days is by fax. Exceptions are such businesses as design services, publishing, film and advertising. If they have drab stationery, the customers may doubt their ability.

### Change-of-address slips

Another item that deserves special attention. They often end up looking like the hurried afterthought they usually are. Yet all suppliers, customers or government bodies will need to know how to make contact. I have received change-of-address slips a week after people have moved!

The first requirement of a good change-of-address slip is that it should attract instant attention when received. It must be different, have lots of punch and, above all, be memorable. A flat note on a thin slip of paper will get lost.

Secondly, it has to be of a shape and design that can be stuck in a date pad, on a notice board, or in a phone book — with the fax and telephone number in bright Day-Glo (TM) ink if necessary.

I've shifted premises about six times in my career. The best change-of-address card we ever used is shown on this page.

### Compliments slips

These usually accompany special documents, parcels and gifts being sent to VIPs or valued customers. They should be tastefully designed to show that they come from a company of good standing and some style.

### Business cards

These are usually too large, too faint, too prosaic and have the wrong typeface. People concentrate too much on the presentation of their names and titles and give little attention to what the company does or the display of the company logo for identification.

The best approach, although few of us might care for it, is to have a photograph added. Then, when arriving home after having met a bewildering number of people, you can at least put a face to a company title.

I confess to more than a few *faux pas*, particularly in Japan and China, when I have written to a Tokardo or Susabi or Wu, Li or Chen, without knowing whether I am addressing the boss or the sales manager — or even a male or a female!

Years ago, when Bill Simmons was the chairman/chief executive of Singapore's Straits Times Press, he attended a newspaper conference in Tokyo. He was surrounded by twenty-five Japanese, all bowing like mechanical toys as they circled the gathering handing out their business cards. Bill joined the parade, handing out his own cards at a frightening rate until he approached another smiling face.

"This is my card," offered Bill.

"No, no, it is my card!", protested the recipient.

In the confusion Bill had gone beyond the full circle and was returning cards to their owners.

A friend of mine with a sense of humour produced a plain card with two words on the front: "My Card". When people would say, "Here is my card," he would respond with, "Here is 'My Card'!" The recipient would get a chuckle out of it but he would remember him because the full and proper information was printed on the reverse.

One of the most innovative business cards I have seen is produced by John Owen of Weldon Owen. It is a tiny booklet, the size of a business card, with twelve pages illustrating his new book titles. It has been produced for many years, with great success.

### Fax paper

The company logo should be well designed for use on a fax. This needs a special approach. For example, if your logo is embossed it will not show up on a fax. More attention should be paid to clear, simple designs for fax paper.

### Envelopes

The company logo should be clearly visible and the envelopes made of strong material. Avoid heavy paper that can contribute to postal costs.

### Invoices and purchase orders

The design must fit the use. It should have clear instructions, items to be purchased or sold, plenty of room for figure work and additions, and enough copies for all concerned. Early in my career, after conducting a simple time and motion study I designed an invoice system that halved the number of staff required in the warehouse. How an invoice looks and functions is very important.

No company, no matter how small, should operate without a properly designed and executed purchase order. I am always astonished by companies which purchase material without proper orders.

### Inter-office memo

I conclude with this enemy of efficiency by saying that if you attack inter-office memos and reduce their number by 70 per cent, your communication and efficiency will improve markedly. Try calculating the hours spent calling in secretaries, dictating memos, receiving memos, adding them to the pile, dictating replies and sending copies to the managing director, the distribution manager, and even the cleaner. You will find that it costs the company a fortune in hours.

## THE LAST WORD — SHOULD YOU WRITE IT AT ALL?

If you considered that the letters, memos or notes that you write might one day appear in a court of law to be read, examined and exposed to the world, you would think twice about what you put on paper.

It *does* happen! It happened to me in 1972, when we were summoned to appear in court to defend a law suit by an author. The managing director of the division directly involved had written a long memo to me providing all the facts, but with no recommendation. I scribbled a hasty (and somewhat testy) note to him at the bottom of the memo: "Christ, what will we do now?". When this was put before the learned judge, he said, "I'm reading your group chief executive's reply, and it appears he was at a bit of a loss as to what to do."

There are many instances around the world when a person's determination to churn out paperwork has caused their corporate demise. So think, and think again, before you put it in writing. Consider talking first. Or make the effort to visit if it is appropriate.

CHAPTER 4

# THE DEAL

Your word is your bond. And everybody else's word
in your company is your bond.

**K.E.W.**

Business begins when two parties get together, one buying, the other selling. These transactions can be multi-million dollar deals, long- or short-term contracts for supply, or a service or consultancy agreement with management consultants, insurance brokers, auditors, merchant bankers or acquisition consultants. The list is endless.

## HEADS OF AGREEMENT

For any deal to be successful, there must be complete understanding by both parties. Much time should be spent determining what I call "the spirit of the deal". The "spirit" may be put together in the first few hours or days, though it might take weeks. From this basic "spirit" a very informal "heads of agreement" should be put together by the parties negotiating. Be cautious about involving attorneys or legal advisers during these stages.

Once the spirit and heads of agreement have been reached, the parties should hand them over to their legal people to put together the formal contracts. The negotiators should give clear instructions that their attorneys must not compromise the spirit of the heads of agreement while formalising the agreement into a legal document.

I have seen many deals turn ugly because the legal people on both sides tampered with the spirit and couched the formal agreement in language that the original negotiators couldn't understand.

*The author concludes a publishing agreement with President Suharto of Indonesia.*

It sounds corny, but for a deal to be successful negotiators must always put themselves in the position of the other person and ask, "Is what I am asking honest, fair and reasonable?" Obviously we are all inclined to answer this question under the influence of self-interest. But if both parties begin with this attitude, they will find that negotiations will loosen up and accelerate considerably.

The 1984 Olympic Games in Los Angeles was a most remarkable commercial venture, a key factor of which was the securing of a multi-million dollar sponsor. The story goes that the chief of the ultimate sponsor, a soft drink company, and the very successful organiser of the Games, sat down at a long table, both sides lined with financial advisers and attorneys. After a brief discussion, the two men agreed to a deal and both signed a blank piece of paper. The advisers on both sides were told to draw up the formal agreement in such a way that it did not break the "spirit" or the good will of the two men who had closed the deal. (This is a rare example where you should have your attorneys in on the first meeting.) The spirit of the agreement was retained and provided the basis for a wonderfully successful event.

## Don't overlook the detail ...

I do not suggest that agreements should not be drawn up in a proper manner, with great attention to detail, but I believe that the lawyers should write the contract in plain English, avoiding ponderous legal language. Both parties must clearly understand all terms and definitions. Most problems occur from differing interpretations. For instance, an item I might regard as properly included in operating overheads might be seen quite differently by the person with whom I am dealing.

## ... But the guts of the deal must be there

I have seen a situation in which both parties used so much intellectual effort drawing up a deal — editing, correcting, and re-editing — that they overlooked the main body of the deal and the reason for it. I discovered after a brief look at both contracts that

*Brilliant American animation artist and businessman Bill Hanna,*
*of Hanna Barbera, seals an agreement with the author to form*
*a joint company in Australia in 1972.*

they had removed the fundamental "spirit" of the deal. This happens much more often than you might imagine.

The definition and language of a deal is even more difficult — and critical — when the contract is between different nationalities.

## A ROGUE WILL ALWAYS CATCH YOU

No matter how careful you are with contracts, if the person you are dealing with is a rogue, you can get caught. We have all been there, and will no doubt be caught again. Obviously, you must take steps to protect yourself by assessing the people you are dealing with in terms of their success, credibility, family honesty and all the normal checks. After that you must hope for the best!

I have always held to a philosophy that you must go through life trusting people to be honest. It is the best way to enjoy an open, fulfilled business life. The contrary view, which afflicts all too many business people, causes them to become paranoid, intense, screwed-up and suspicious of everyone they meet.

## GUARD YOUR OWN INTEGRITY

Your word is your bond, and everybody else's word in your company is your bond. I am a great believer in this old principle, even if circumstances suddenly change. This does not mean, however, that if caught in a deal that has become very sticky you cannot go back to the other party, explain the problem, and request a change.

It's important to explain your commitment to integrity to everyone in your organisation. If people who work for you break their word, people will ultimately conclude that you are also dishonest, though you may be quite ignorant of the matter.

Those of us who have been in senior management will have been shocked on many occasions to discover that people down the line have made devious or dishonest deals. Even worse, they may claim their actions are a result of your policy!

I've suffered the discomfort of sitting in a restaurant overhearing staff who had not yet met me tell a customer how difficult, mean and lacking in compassion I was in business. I made it known to them the next day that I had overheard the conversation and how affronted I was. In future, I said, they should have the courtesy and the common sense to enquire directly about the boss's way of conducting business before spouting hearsay.

## A DEAL IS A DEAL

Some years ago, one of my managers placed a $500 000 order with an English publisher by phone and sent a telex as confirmation. Because of major cash flow problems some weeks later, the manager cancelled the order, using the disingenuous excuse that it had not been binding because it had never been placed on our official order form.

Needless to say, the principals of the company phoned me to complain that they had committed themselves and were, quite naturally, very upset. I promised to investigate the matter and quickly get back to them. When I discovered the truth of it I told the manager we would proceed with the order because not only had he given his word, but he had, indirectly, also given mine. I phoned the supplier, admitting our mistake. I explained that it was a very large commitment in our present cash position and that it would help ease the pressure if we could split deliveries and payments over twelve months. This solution was not only acceptable to both sides, but preserved a successful business relationship that lasted twenty-five years.

It would be naïve to suggest that dishonesty doesn't exist in business. I know of many people, not quite men of their word, who went on to achieve success of a rather dubious kind. Unfortunately, these days, managers, staff and the public have come to believe that to be successful and make a lot of money you have to be hard, unfair or downright dishonest. Certainly, there is evidence enough that many get there this way. I, nevertheless, rejoice in the knowledge that there are many more successful people in life who, in the main, have done the right thing by their customers and their employees.

The greatest personal satisfaction a business person can have is to be able to look directly into the proverbial mirror and feel no misgivings about his or her integrity.

# CHAPTER 5

# TRADING IN ANOTHER STATE OR COUNTRY

Go with an open mind and a friendly spirit. Learn all about
the country and its people. Remember you are a guest.
And good guests always consider their hosts.

**K.E.W.**

Foreigners rarely comprehend how difficult it is to run businesses across the vast states and territories of Australia. Sydney and Perth, for instance, are nearly as far apart as London and Moscow, with practically no population in between.

## WHICH STATE?

Tradition or history, rather than more practical considerations, have led companies to establish their head offices and distribution centres in the different states. Modern businesses need to be more flexible than this. The fact is, it is more costly to run particular businesses in some states than in others. Apart from government charges or the cost of local labour, the proximity of your market must be considered. Some states even offer to subsidise companies prepared to establish themselves there.

Labour can also be easier to source in some states. For example, some see the sunny Queensland lifestyle, when compared to that of colder southern states, as a drawcard for employees. Such advantages deserve serious consideration.

The principles of conducting business interstate can be applied to almost every country in the world.

*To celebrate the book* Salute to Singapore, *all Singaporeans born
25 years earlier — the year the ruling Peoples' Action Party was founded —
were invited to a local stadium. The author, pictured saluting the throng, was
astonished to find himself having to entertain more than 20 000 people!*

# USA

Many companies fail to establish themselves in the US market
because they treat it as a single entity instead of as a collection of
different business environments with a complex mix of local laws,
controls, taxes, lifestyles, and cultural and ethnic backgrounds.
Each of the fifty states should be treated separately when
establishing a business there.

Let's take New York. New York City is a world in its own right, with a large population comprising almost every ethnic group crammed into the biggest business centre in the world. New York oversees more than one-third of the world's Gross National Product. Big business decisions here are the norm rather than the exception. But that's the Big Apple and you have got to understand that doing business in New York is very different from doing business in California.

The Californian ethos evolved as a result of a big shift in the US population in the 1940s, as eastern staters followed the sun in pursuit of the "Hollywood Dream". In their wake came developers and entrepreneurs, instant billionaires, who tailored their product and their approach quite specifically to this new American lifestyle. The Lane family of publishers is an excellent example. Their *Sunset* magazine and books captured the special mood, the lifestyle and the environment of the new Californians.

The reality is that every state is, to varying degrees, different from the next. If you start with this attitude and accept that you must attack your market patiently, one state at a time, you can do very well in the USA. But to take on the US as a whole, with its different attitudes and vast distances, is an almost impossible task.

## UNITED KINGDOM

Here again, to assume that doing business in Scotland is the same as doing it in Wales or England is folly. Call a Welshman or a Scot an Englishman and see how successful you are! Even within England, business practices in the Midlands are almost as far removed from those in the south as England's are from France (ignoring language for a moment).

## THE AUSTRALIAN ATTITUDE

When Geoffrey Blainey wrote the *The Tyranny of Distance* in the 1960s, he described Australia's biggest hurdle perfectly. We are 27 000 kilometres from the centre of English-speaking civilisation. We are, in the words of the Aboriginal author, Eric Wilmot, "the last great experiment". Together with New Zealand we are an isolated pocket of predominantly white, English-speaking peoples at the edge of the vast populations of Asia. Our closest neighbour, Indonesia, has a population of about 150 million people. We must accept that it will always be difficult for our sparsely-populated and culturally-isolated country to develop business and cultural relationships beyond its own massive territory.

## Our own culture

Like any young nation, we are still struggling to develop our own culture and understand our unique environment. The experience is not unlike that of a young family starting a new life in an isolated area. While building a farm the family must protect, feed, educate and house the children. In time it must improve its means of production to generate enough income to buy bigger farms that will accommodate the next generation and fulfil the normal dreams of success. The pioneer may possess the vision to ensure success despite inevitable setbacks. The mixed experiences of success, adversity and occasional tragedy will gradually breed a tradition.

Australia is a nation of immigrants and a unique indigenous people. We have all the problems of blending ourselves into an homogenous group, while still appreciating both where we've come from and, more importantly, where we're headed.

Now, just as the Portuguese, the Dutch and the British once urged their bold seafarers to seek out trade in remote parts — and we were always the end of the line — so we must now traverse those routes back to *their* home markets. I suspect it will take no less faith, courage and tenacity for us to prevail along these "reverse" trade routes, despite the advantage of considerably better ships!

We must come to terms with all these things and tackle the following objectives with a will:

- Every product we produce should be the best in the world in terms of quality and value. Government and the community must support and take pride in that product and the image it projects, like the Swedes with the Volvo and Saab, the Danes with Jensen, the French with their wines and the Concorde and the Dutch with their cheeses and electronics.

- We must rediscover our courage to invest time and money in contemporary industries and research and development. We must accept that digging holes, felling trees and exporting non-renewable resources has failed us. So-called developing countries, such as Indonesia and Malaysia, have their own large-scale petrochemical industries, while we have stopped developing a petrochemical plant in Western Australia.
- Governments must remove excessive tax imposts on companies that have the ability to develop exports and build successful offshore businesses for Australia.
- As a nation, and as traders, we are a small part of a fiercely competitive global environment. We must acknowledge that it is not the "level playing field" absurdly promoted by government ministers, academics and bureaucrats. How can Australia, a country so weak in trade, naïvely seek to create a level playing field at home when dealing with countries with thousands of years' experience as merchants and traders who will, when it suits their interests, negotiate separate and exclusive deals (under the table if necessary) to keep their money and product flowing? For example, the fabled level playing field for the Japanese is: "Let us sell our excellent products in your large domestic market (such as the USA, England and developing countries such as Indonesia and Malaysia), but, I'm so sorry, we cannot let you join the fierce competition of our domestic market. That is for us alone!".
- We must learn to negotiate a trade deal with strength and dignity. We mustn't plead or kowtow, especially when being criticised or screwed by prospective trading partners. We have to be prepared to be hard. To hold our breath and walk away from a poor deal. To be patient, but determined. And we must imbue the smallest business person and farmer with this spirit.

A classic example of our weakness in business is evident in our dealings with the Japanese. Before we even start, the Department of Trade — the so-called experts — warns us that we must do nothing in negotiations that might embarrass the Japanese or push them into a corner where they might lose face. This immediately gives our Japanese counterparts an enormous advantage in any trading deal. As a result our negotiators, instead of being determined and confident, are so terrified of offending that they can hardly close a deal. Australians should take the view that we, too, are a proud people: we must stand tall and allow no-one to strip us of our dignity.

By the same token, we should admire — as I do — Japan's success. Their great objective as one nation is to produce innovative, quality products at prices that create volume sales. And, not content with initial success, they will continually refine that product, polishing the gem.

## How to behave in other countries

If I have voiced some criticisms of the Japanese, let me quickly point out that few of us are without fault in foreign lands. The business people of many nations, including Australia — and for that matter people who simply work or live abroad — are inclined to be smug about the negative qualities of that country from the moment they arrive. They compare any shortcomings with the positive qualities of their own country. Myopic as this is, it is relatively inoffensive compared with the arrogance of then spruiking the virtues of one's own culture, instead of having the grace and intelligence to appreciate the culture of the host. I have had a home in Bali for many, many years and have often despaired of the crassness of visitors to that beautiful island.

My advice to all who venture to live or conduct business in foreign parts is simply this: Go with an open mind and a friendly spirit. Learn all about the country and its people. Remember you are a guest. And good guests always consider their hosts.

CHAPTER 6

# ADVERTISING AND PROMOTION

*Mate, you're crazy! $6.95 is still a bargain and*
*I'll spend the extra $2 to put it on television for you.*

JOHN SINGLETON

I've got nothing against advertising agencies. Quite the contrary. At their best they are brilliant. But I am continually disappointed by some elements in the conduct of business between agency and client.

Experience tells me that advertising agency personnel cannot possibly share their client's enthusiasm for containing costs — especially from their own subcontractors. Any printer, picture library owner, typesetter or artist will tell you that they can charge advertising agencies much more than any other client and get away with it.

This applies particularly to film production houses producing cinema or television ads. Some production ventures seem like vehicles for egos with a yen to create a Hollywood extravaganza rather than a 30-second commercial. They reel in a cast of thousands, expensive locations and sets, and ring up astonishing hotel and travel costs. Yet when the ad goes to air, you find yourself straining to discern what should be crystal clear — the product, what it offers, where you get it and how much it costs!

Powerful companies with one brand image to project, such as Coca-Cola, Pepsi, or Ford Motor Company, are in a different category. No doubt they can justify the time and expense of such advertising. But I have seen many companies spend in excess of $500 000 creating a series of TV commercials when their annual profits are only $1.5 million!

## Agencies profit from your costs

Almost every advertising agency in the world has been pulled back dramatically in the 1990s, though I assume the principle that they receive a percentage of all costs the client spends on advertising still applies.

What has always been needed is a totally different arrangement in which the agency becomes more a part of the company and the company feels more involved with the agency. They should share a simple, common goal — to produce the right product and put it in the right place, at the right time, at the right price, with the right promotion. (If I labour this elsewhere in the book it's intentional, because it is my most urgent message in marketing.)

Over almost four decades I have been involved in hundreds of advertising campaigns. Since the advent of the word processor, probably 75 per cent of the agency's presentation is usually pre-digested garbage stored in the word processor. The same garbage is handed out to every client, with about 25 per cent added which relates specifically to *your* product. Presentations, accompanied by the usual razzmatazz, waft on with a rising tide of esoteric gobbledygook till the client is so engulfed, confused or overawed that they can only manage a "hmm" or an "err" before capitulating. Business people rarely speak the same language as advertising people and are afraid to look foolish if they protest too loudly.

You cannot blame the agency for trying to make a profit. Responsibility remains with the client, who must be firm. They must be sure the agency understands what the product is all about and then give an unequivocal "Yes" or "No" when it comes to costs.

## Thank God for agencies

Having advanced a negative view, it is important to add that many businesses and products would never have succeeded, or even reached the market, without the genius of someone in an advertising agency. It may have been the account executive, the copywriter, the jingle creator, the brilliant layout artist, or the guy down the line who simply says, "You're kidding! I thought you'd do it this way." I'll give a few examples of how the genius of an advertising agency has helped in my career.

## Books on TV

In 1969, my young advertising promotion manager at the Hamlyn Group, Neil Balnaves, introduced me to a company called Spasm, which I thought was the nickname of one of the partners, John Singleton. In fact, it was the initials of all the partners — Singleton, Palmer, Strauss and McCallum.

A very young John Singleton arrived with a presentation to show me how he could sell more product for me. He looked at a new fishing book we were going to put on the market. It was a 1000-page book for $4.95. Amazing value, even in those days.

"Mate, you're crazy: $6.95 is still a bargain and I'll spend the extra two dollars to put it on television for you," said Singleton.

It seemed reasonable and clever. The only problem was that nobody in the world had ever promoted a book on television before. John found a magnificent, bearded fisherman and put him on television saying, "Here it is! One thousand pages of my personal experiences on how to catch fish. Any father that doesn't teach his kid to fish is no father at all!"

Whooosh! 50 000 copies sold overnight. A roaring best-seller. We were on our way, John and I. Our next big project was *Australia's Heritage,* a huge publishing venture into partworks — so big, in fact, that it would have closed down the Hamlyn Group in Australia if it had failed. In 1970, a commitment of $267 000 was made on TV over a ten-day period, which would be about $2.2 million in today's figures.

What did John do that was pure genius?

Firstly, of all the people he could have got as a presenter, he strongly recommended Paul Hamlyn for this aggressively nationalistic Australian publication. Here was a rather aesthetic-looking man with a distinctly British upper-class accent and a slight lisp. Hardly the quintessential Australian one might have expected!

Secondly, he produced the first one-and-a-half minute commercial.

*NSW State Governor, Sir Roden Cutler, presents the Hoover Award*
*for marketing to the author. The project which won the award,*
Australia's Heritage, *resulted in 7.8 million copies sold.*

Thirdly, he advised against spreading the exposure over all channels like everyone else. "Let's get the best deal from the country's lowest-rating station," he said. "We'll saturate the audience on Channel 10." He assured us that Ian Clelland (Channel 10, Sydney) would put his weight behind it.

And fourthly, despite the product having been completed, he said: "Listen mate, history is okay but shit, what the parents want is a bloody book their kids can cut up for school projects." So we rushed to add a double page of study projects for cut-outs in the centrefold of the book so that it could also be advertised on television with the wall charts, and other things.

The result? The most successful publishing venture Australia had seen to date, with no less than 7.8 million units sold over a two-year period. We received the Hoover Award for the most outstanding piece of marketing in Australia and, boy, did it make money! More than twenty years later this product — updated — is still being sold successfully by my company. Singo hasn't done too badly himself.

The point I want to stress is the benefit of a successful relationship between a client and its advertising agency. In this instance it produced a hugely effective sales technique which we employed to similar effect with future products. Using the same approach, *Australia's Wildlife Heritage* sold 5.8 million copies and *New Zealand's Heritage* 5.9 million copies. There is no way that this promotion and marketing technique could have evolved without our association with an advertising agency, and without John Singleton in particular.

Years later I worked with Geoffrey Wilde, the head of the NSW office of Clemengers advertising agency. Geoff, conservative and thorough as he was, was nevertheless a warm person who cared a lot about people. At the time I had spoken to Peter Luck, who was working as a reporter on a segment of the "Four Corners" current affairs program called "Corner Five". He was young and talented, but disillusioned with the ABC. I suggested I back him in a project, give him an office, and away we go. He said he'd like to research the archives of all the old film in Australia to put together a series of books.

We worked on it for a month before deciding that it would make a better TV documentary series. Yet, struggle as we might, we couldn't come up with a satisfactory title for the series. When we discussed the issue with Geoffrey he said: "Hell, I thought you were going to call it 'This Fabulous Century' like the US series 'Our Fabulous Century'. "

Geoff got it in one. We did it. And it went on to win the award for Best Documentary of the Year. Launched at the same time as the enormously popular "60 Minutes" program, it belted the backside off it in the ratings.

Yes, you sure as hell need a good agency.

# CHAPTER 7

# MARKETING: MY DEFINITION

Put the right product in the right place at the right time
at the right price with the right promotion.

**K.E.W.**

I start this chapter in the knowledge that even my fundamental definition of marketing is going to be challenged. As long ago as my business school days I argued with fellow students about it, and my tutors undoubtedly considered failing me for my perverse view. Nevertheless, my definition has helped me create successful marketing companies around the world. So, here it is:

> Marketing encompasses the activity of sales, promotion and distribution. Its function is to put the right product in the right place at the right time at the right price with the right promotion.

I believe, therefore, that the marketing function starts when a product is delivered into the arms of the sales team. Not before.

Like many others, my erstwhile financial adviser, Simon Gompertz, utterly disagrees. He believes marketing starts with the earliest concept, and then moves on through the development, manufacture or process, promotion, and sales and distribution functions. I argued that he might as well include every function in business. "Yes," he said, "excluding only two functions — financing and what might loosely be called financial services."

## THE RIGHT PRODUCT

The right product may start as a concept of random inspiration or as the result of feedback from the ultimate user. Either way, it must fit the needs of marketing. The concept is then developed and manufactured to achieve innovative quality at a predetermined price. Manufacturing/production delivers this product to the

*We strove to make our book launchings a little different at the Hamlyn Group.
Here Margaret Fulton's* Italian Cookbook *is launched aboard
a special Alitalia flight over Sydney and Melbourne.*

*A ground-breaking marketing concept introduced by the author while chief executive
of the Hamlyn Group was the "in-store" department, wherein Hamlyn books
were presented in their own section within a large department store.
This one was in Farmers in Sydney.*

marketing services. In other words, the manufacturing arm must provide what is required by the marketing function.

## THE RIGHT PLACE

The right place is determined by the marketing department as a whole. It may choose to sell directly to the consumer, or to sell through retail outlets or a variety of other distribution systems.

## THE RIGHT TIME

The timing must also be right. It may be influenced by the seasons or special gift-giving periods, such as Christmas, Father's Day, Mother's Day, or other days of special celebration. It is the manufacturing/production function to make sure the finished product is available for marketing at the right time.

## THE RIGHT PRICE

The right price is really what the market will stand. A very low price need not be the right price. For, if you come in below your competitors' prices, it will only be a matter of time before they reduce theirs to compete. Accordingly, you should have something up your sleeve in anticipation of such a move. As a rule, innovative products offer more flexibility in determining a retail price point.

(The right price is one area where Gompertz's argument that manufacturing is part of marketing gains credence, because, as far as I'm concerned, it is the responsibility of the manufacturing unit to ensure that the cost of the product does not exceed that expected by the marketing department.)

## THE RIGHT PROMOTION

It's no good putting the right product in the right place at the right time at the right price if no-one knows about it! This marketing function is obvious. I don't believe that packaging should be decided by the manufacturing/production department. It should be a function of marketing, though there are many grey areas. In book publishing, for instance, book jackets are usually the province of editorial (manufacturing) and rarely decided by marketing.

In summary, when I describe a product as marketing driven, I simply mean that it has conformed with all the steps laid out above. In book publishing, many international companies are still editorial (manufacturing) driven. It is not my philosophy and we couldn't survive in some divisions if we relied solely on editorial driven decisions.

With the speed of new technology, marketing will probably come to encompass many more functions. Perhaps, when Simon and I are dead and buried, his definition might be closer to the mark after all.

*Bob Hawke and the author at the launch of the* Great Australian Annual.

# CHAPTER 8

# QUALITY: THE ENDLESS PURSUIT OF EXCELLENCE

Good enough is never good enough.

**K.E.W.**

The first doctrine of production should be quality, whatever the product. This does not mean that we shouldn't produce to a price, but it does mean that we must inject quality *relative* to that price. This should be self-evident. No company will survive for long if it doesn't get this right. How often have we seen similar products, made in the same country, at the same price — one with obvious quality and the other shoddy? The shoddy one will ultimately disappear, however vigorously it is pushed in the market.

Increasingly, consumers around the world are demanding quality for their money. If a company wants to secure business in the wider global community, it must be assiduous in quality control. This is an absolute must. Any company that ignores the fact will not be around in the year 2000.

Start by encouraging those in the front line to understand how important quality is for their survival. Management must also be taught the importance of quality in supervising and maintaining the highest standards. Even more important is the need for continuous training of all staff. They must be convinced that their role — *no matter how small* — plays a significant part in the ultimate success of the product. You don't achieve quality merely by installing someone at the end of a production line to check the goods. Reliable quality is achieved by creating a genuinely committed attitude in all staff. They must feel committed and confident enough to be able to boast to friends, "We produce the best ... in the world!"

Moreover, companies that produce quality products usually benefit from a commensurate lift in staff morale. The workers are proud to belong. Not surprisingly, workers at a company that produces inferior goods will suffer low morale and take little pride in their work. The inevitable outcome is more shoddy goods.

To achieve the desired result, there has to be a workplace culture that refuses to compromise on quality at any level. This means a quality performance from staff, suppliers and subcontractors. Standards start there. If we accept shoddy work at the lowest level, or from other sources, it will surely create problems down the line.

Quality must also be achieved in both distribution and after-sales service. Even good products will fail if poorly marketed. And the very best will suffer from a poor after-sales service.

I have seen some wonderfully innovative Australian products that don't quite make it. Not because of promotion, sales, or even distribution, but because the producers failed to make that extra effort to achieve better quality than the competition.

## INNOVATION

Quality and innovation go hand in hand. If you are continually innovative your product will remain less price-sensitive and more attractive than your competitor's. One of the reasons for the remarkable rise of Japanese industry is its genuine commitment to innovation. One day they produce a marvellous automatic camera. The next time round they've made it waterproof. As European car manufacturers struggle to match the myriad of gadgets their Japanese counterparts offer, the Japanese car makers are moving on — installing solar panels in the roof which drive the air conditioner while the car is parked in the sun. If price is not a factor, then there is no doubt which car will attract the consumer. But the quality must be there. Innovation in a second-rate product will excite only passing interest.

## PRESENTATION OF QUALITY

A quality product not only deserves a quality presentation, it *needs* it. How often have we seen fine products camouflaged at the seduction stage by poor packaging and presentation? A quality image needs to be forcefully projected to convince the consumer that the product behind the packaging is as good as you claim. You are unlikely to achieve this by skimping on presentation.

I've been in companies that have produced a wonderful quality product after having spent millions on development. They have then put the entire investment at risk by skimping on the promotional artwork and packaging.

Appearance is not the only factor in packaging. The goods must travel well. Who wants a product that is damaged by the time they've got it home?

## DAMAGE CONTROL

While on the subject of damaged goods, there should always be a system to promptly replace damaged units, with minimum inconvenience to the consumer. This is the only proper response for a quality business, though you might already have lost your customer.

In 1969 I published the Hamlyn *Encyclopedic World Dictionary* in Australia. At the time it was the most dramatically different dictionary in the world. It was well promoted and sold in vast numbers very quickly. I happened to walk into the Hamlyn reception one morning to find a little old lady arguing with our receptionist. When I interceded she told the following story. Having bought our dictionary at Farmers department store, she discovered a section in the middle was upside down. (For those who don't know the business, as many as 2000 copies in a print run of 50 000 might be misbound, sometimes more. This one had obviously got through quality control!) When she returned the book an attendant in the book department told her it was the fault of the publisher. When she rang our office she was told that if she brought it to our head office at Dee Why we would replace it.

This woman lived in Sutherland, fully 35 kilometres away. After catching four buses she finally arrived at our reception, only to be told by our receptionist that it really was the retailer's responsibility. This may be hard to believe, but it happens. Here was a woman who, having been convinced to buy our wonderful dictionary, was now copping a right royal runaround for her faith.

No-one was responding with common sense, let alone business acumen. I gave her six dictionaries for relatives, a pile of other Hamlyn books, and put her in a taxi back to Sutherland. The printers who had stuffed up their quality control shared the cost!

So, if you do let something through — and it happens — immediately over-compensate the poor customer. Some companies, or their staff, dig their heels in to the point of stupidity. It may be difficult to introduce, but it is important that the front line be given the power to use their initiative to protect the quality image of the company. They should not feel obliged to seek middle management's permission.

An attitude of quality in production and service should permeate from the managing director to the cleaner. Good enough is *never* good enough.

# CHAPTER 9

# THE BOARD OF DIRECTORS

*If I was really honest with myself, I didn't contribute much
in those eight years as a director of a major public company.
It was really eight years of wasted time.*

**K.E.W.**

We see two main types of boards in companies around the world. There are others, such as institutional boards and charitable boards, but I confine my observations to the "paper" boards and "executive" boards.

## THE "PAPER" BOARD

The "paper" board is usually comprised of a chief executive of the group plus the chief executives of divisions, sometimes with a sprinkling of outside directors, sometimes with an outside chairman or a chief executive chairman. Why a "paper" board? Because when a divisional chief executive/director runs up against the group chief executive and/or chairman who controls the board, how can they realistically challenge the head honcho? Are they going to be comfortable taking on the boss in front of the board, with all their counterparts listening in? Not likely! Not if they've got a modicum of common sense.

So, in the end, debate is choked off and the paperwork that comes before the board will be rubber stamped. Of course, divisional chiefs will want to upstage their peers through erudite criticism of proposals from other divisions. But they are not really going to change the destiny of the group as "mere" directors.

I was such a director of one of Australia's largest public companies years ago. On my departure I was quoted in the press as saying, "If I was really honest with myself, I didn't contribute much in those eight years as a director. It was really eight years of wasted time." The only issue I took a firm stand on came right at the end of my tenure, when Reed Consolidated Industries was advised that Hardie's takeover offer was a very good one. I felt it should have been better and, from memory, it was subsequently increased. Along with Keith Davenport, the chief executive, and financial chief David Say, I also pushed hard to ensure that anybody made redundant by the takeover would be properly compensated. In the event, Davenport and Say did a brilliant job with the parent group in England to ensure that a proper fund was created for this purpose.

But, all in all, we were just a paper board, the more so because our decision-making was limited by a parent board in England. We went along with the chairman and chief in practically everything we did, always conscious of our parent board. As I sat there over the eight years I often wondered whether the group would be better served by an individual owner instead of a board. I felt that the group would probably be stronger without our board. Certainly, decision making would have been quicker and more flexible. I came to this conclusion after experiencing delays and frustrations while the chief executive of Reed Paper Products decided on or sought approval for new building, new machinery, or new direction. By contrast, the opposition, Smorgens, was a family-owned company which made its decisions quickly and left Reed Paper Products far behind. We were still debating what should be done twelve months after Smorgens had done it.

Paper boards, I'm afraid, linger somewhere between the inefficient and the superfluous. They should be avoided at all costs.

## OUTSIDE DIRECTORS

The solution is not always to be found in outside directors, either. An outside director sat next to me on an aircraft one day. "Oh, damn," he grumbled, "I've brought the BHP briefcase instead of the Reed briefcase." He was a director of ten leading corporations and kept a briefcase for each, which his secretary would dutifully fill in preparation for his next board meeting. With this sort of load perhaps he couldn't be blamed for occasionally wondering whether he was examining a proposal for a steel mill or a wallpaper-making machine. I gained an uneasy feeling that some of his learned comments might be repeated verbatim about any proposal that might arise at each of his ten boards.

Despite my misgivings about professional directors, there are some obvious benefits. Their experience and knowledge can be invaluable to a board, particularly when it comes to such issues as institutional manoeuvring. It may simply be an ability to pick up a telephone and get the ear of a Prime Minister or a captain of industry. Nevertheless, I'm sure these same people would be just as happy to receive a consultancy fee for occasional advice rather than have to sit through boring board meetings.

Another important asset for a board is an experienced chairman. Our chairman at Reed was an honest, upright man who was able to field questions at shareholders' meetings with reassuring authority. His reputation was such that he enjoyed the respect of the establishment back in England — which gave us poor operating blokes reasonable protection from London.

## The executive, hands-on board

My definition of an executive board differs sharply from most textbook conventions. An executive board, to my way of thinking, is simply one comprised of non-executive outside directors or chief operating executives, each with equal status and authority to make decisions by a majority vote. Those decisions are *absolutely* final. Such board members must be chosen for their experience; they should represent a balance of youth and maturity; they may own their own companies, and they should know how to manage and make decisions. This board must also be able to convene swiftly and make quick decisions. It must be flexible enough to match the owner's vigour and pace.

Such boards should be energetic, visionary and direct. They should be compassionate, too, for without this quality they will ultimately fail their company. They must also ensure adherence to the group's mission statement or, in the absence of a statement, the broad thrust of the company's philosophy.

The executive board seems to be preferred in family-owned

companies and sole proprietorships because its day-to-day involvement provides checks and balances between the chief executive and the operating units. Regrettably, we don't find this sort of structure too often with the larger public companies.

If one looks at the crash of some large corporations in Australia, a large question mark continues to hang over the credibility of some prominent board members. Some didn't have the guts to properly discharge their responsibilities. Others were so naïve or dumb that they clearly didn't have the qualifications to take on the responsibilities of directorship in the first place. Where are these directors now? Don't be surprised to find many of them still sitting on boards of large companies: nothing much changes in the smoky atmosphere of the directors' club. I'm not suggesting dishonesty, but I question the competency of their performance in light of the demise of large companies and the massive losses to shareholders.

Directors have grave responsibilities under law, yet I'm often confronted by people anxious to become directors because it sounds good, bestows status, or for a host of other wrong reasons. I suspect some seek directorships of our leading companies for the same reasons, though the remuneration may have some influence. My advice to young people is that they need a directorship like a hole in the head. Maybe one day we will re-define both the term and the role to properly describe what we expect from those in this position.

## THE DIRECTOR'S APPROACH

There are two types of director. There's the very conservative, very proper establishment director, who enjoys the solemnity of his or her elevated position. They are often so removed from the real world and the company's markets that they are little better than useless. The other type are more down to earth and have risen through the ranks by virtue of their talents as decision makers and achievers. Such people can move the whole board to action with sheer energy and drive. I've met a few of this type — senior people who were a great help to me in my own business career.

I have had the honour of serving on charity boards with some great directors of this ilk. They had brilliant intellects, charitable natures and a sense of humour. They were also decisive doers. I would embarrass such directors by naming them, but as I sat on one of these boards one day it dawned on me that no large corporation in the world could gather round a table the brain power these directors had brought to a small charity. Unfortunately the head man in America was oblivious to this, believing he had a distinguished rubber stamp. It was a costly mistake because he lost them all in the end. Such men were not to be taken lightly.

## OF LESSER MEN IN DARK BLUE SUITS ...

Snobbery raises its snout from time to time in the business of directorships.

The establishment was recently shocked when the Conrad Black syndicate Tourang, owners of the Fairfax Group, appointed advertising guru John Singleton to its board. Some directors of creditors AMP and Westpac objected strongly. Allow me to put forward an opposing view.

Whatever John Singleton's faults, he knows people. He is one of the few men who can throw a party and invite the local football team as well as the Prime Minister and captains of industry. There might also be the odd bookmaker or spruiker from Kings Cross. This same John Singleton can identify when a big company is directing itself into real danger. And he certainly has the guts to call things as they are, without worrying about his reputation among his peers. (In fact, he is such a maverick that you'd need to be a magician to identify John Singleton's peer group. It's certainly not the advertising establishment.) If he'd been on the Westpac board a few years back I have no doubt he would have been the first to sniff trouble. And he would certainly have had the guts to say to the same board which later objected to his Fairfax appointment, "Hey, I think we've got a problem. We're going to lose sales and it could be bad publicity."

Providing the establishment directors can relax a bit, the John Singletons of this world may prove better directors than they imagined. I admit to some ambivalence, however, because if Singleton had stayed on the Fairfax board too long it might have eventually compromised his maverick spirit. It's a bit like the rebel

Dick Smith, who had great success dismantling the bureaucracy when he became head of the Civil Aviation Authority. Yet, despite his protests, he got to be a little more like the CAA every day till he left. The same things happen when union people join a board. No matter how hard they try, over a period they will cease to be effective union representatives because they become *de facto* management.

The underlying lesson to me in all this is: Don't keep the same board too long. Give directors a short term, shake the place up, and move them on.

CHAPTER 10

# THE STATUTORY CHAINS THAT BIND US

*For bureaucracy feeds itself gluttonously.
It is the nature of the beast to swell.*

K.E.W.

Bureaucracies are growing around the world on a massive scale. Even in the former Soviet Union, where the abject failure of a crushing bureaucracy has been exposed for all the world to see, I suspect parts of it are very much alive and others simply dormant. The disgraced bureaucrats are merely waiting for the new order to break down so that they might rise again. For bureaucracy feeds itself gluttonously. It is the nature of the beast to swell. And it is almost impossible to trim, because as one part is slashed, another part takes over. Only the names change.

I share the belief that the global growth of bureaucracy must be reversed and inflexible bureaucratic mentality expunged if the economies of the world are to expand. Perhaps bureaucracies are doomed by their own bloated form. I tend to agree with writer Alvin Toffler, who believes that in future any companies that are formed into bureaucracies — indeed the bureaucracy itself — will eventually simply wither because they will be unable to function with the necessary flexibility.

## GOVERNMENT BUREAUCRACIES

Our government bureaucracies do more to stifle success than any recessionary trend. They are closely followed by our non-government bureaucracies, among them banks and large insurance companies. In evidence I list the following as some of the organisations and departments to which an ordinary, medium-sized business must report:

- State Government Payroll Tax
- Federal Government Corporate Taxation
- Federal Government Securities
- National Securities Commission
- Sales Tax
- Department of Labour and Industry
- Attorney General's Department regarding Registrations
- Federal Government Department of Trade
- Department of Transport
- State and Federal Government Registration
- Medical Benefits
- Compensation Board
- State Government Water and Sewerage
- State Government Land Tax

Then there are the Local Municipal Controls:

- Garbage Rates Controls
- Council Inspections

These are just a few items on a list that seems endless. Nor does it end there. Inspectors can knock on the door to check books, records, registrations and so on.

## Statutory controls

Nearly every business in Australia has an expense called Statutory Requirements. And it is quite an expense. These requirements — company minutes, annual returns and annual tax returns — have grown steadily over the years, adding ceaseless paperwork. They exist so that central bureaucracies can monitor and control companies to prevent them from breaking the law, embezzling funds, or cheating the government, the staff and the customers.

### Company minutes

Few companies note these down accurately for fear of being held to account in the future. It would be interesting to see how the Westpac minutes have changed since their paperwork crucified them.

### Annual returns

These are costly to business, though they help in gathering information on directors and companies. Dunn & Bradstreet should have the returns as a special department!

### Annual tax return

I believe Australians are basically honest. But this trait has come under pressure over the past twenty years in response to rapacious governments increasing indirect, direct and personal taxes. Management, staff and ordinary people have raised their efforts to evade taxation, with all kinds of offshore trickery, deals, cash exchanges and barter deals.

The Tax Department has responded with a vendetta. Too many of us know what it is like to have the company suddenly torn apart by Company Tax Inspectors. Unfortunately, the number of successful prosecutions that have flowed from their investigations suggest that the morality and honesty of our nation is slipping.

Let me say that there is a big difference between minimising the tax a company should pay and avoiding it completely. I do not for a moment condone tax evasion. At the same time, I believe some of the tax imposts levied on businesses border on the unconscionable. For instance, the practice of making businesses pay tax in advance is alone responsible for hindering the progress of some, and hastening the demise of others.

In my opinion, these statutory controls have failed miserably over the past thirty years. Yet they have forced honest companies — the vast majority — to suffer external controls designed for rogues. The only solution is to start again. And keep it simple this time.

## THE OVER-TAXED NATIONAL CONSCIENCE

History shows that when a society is over-taxed and over-governed, it will ultimately collapse. Recent events in Australia reinforce this.

The more the population has been taxed, the more dishonest, disillusioned, and resentful it has become. This nexus must be broken. The Government needs to start from scratch to make taxation so simple and fair that we share the burden equitably. That alone would discourage the dishonesty that's become a part of our culture. This is why I support the concept of paying tax as you purchase. The cheats cannot escape this.

At present the Taxation Department quite properly sees its role as doing everything possible to collect more taxes. However, with the recent decision to increase the department's staff by 15 per cent, it is inviting grim comparison with King John's unfortunate precedent of committing more soldiers to raid more villages to collect more money. This is hardly the way to lead a great, young, exciting nation into the future.

Can this seriously be regarded as a step towards a reconciliation of the country into "One Nation"? Already I know of disgruntled people who are determined to outwit the Taxation Department, with few qualms about dishonesty. For those hard-working business people who pay their dues, these continual incursions into their companies — companies which are employing people and trying to build exports while struggling to keep going in difficult times — are close to the last straw. It creates a form of police state with raids, commissions, boards of investigation and so on.

Let's face it, the Tax Act was most successful twenty-five years ago when it was comparatively simple. Even twenty years ago, when I was chairman of Butterworths Legal Publishers, Ted Mannix's definitive book *Australian Corporate Taxation* ran to a single, slim volume. Now the Tax Act requires more than fifteen large volumes. Even the experts (including the Taxation Department) don't really understand it. How often does it fall to some learned judge to make a decision relating to the Act? And that decision is based on law, which might have nothing to do with fairness.

## THE REAL COSTS

During a discussion about Australia's export potential with then-Minister for Trade, Neal Blewett, I suggested the government total all statutory costs, such as government and municipal charges, holiday loadings, pay roll taxes and training charges, and compare them with those borne by similar companies operating in Hong Kong, Singapore, Taiwan, Japan, San Francisco, New York, Paris, Madrid, Glasgow, London, Dublin and Frankfurt. It hasn't been done yet, but I am sure it would show how much more Australian companies pay in bureaucratic charges while trying to compete in the world market. If the Australian government removed them it would go a long way towards creating that fabled "level playing field" which its ministers are always lauding.

The only solution is to overhaul and simplify business taxation. The federal, state and local governments — in consultation with business — should quickly re-draft a new arrangement to reduce excessive costs, remove some charges altogether, and rid the system of paperwork that serves no purpose.

It can't be done? The bureaucratic and political forces against this are too entrenched? Of course it can. And it must.

# "UNIONS ARE RUINING THE COUNTRY!" NONSENSE!

*Today I see people in unions who are not only well educated,
but often better qualified than the management
with which they must deal.*

**K.E.W.**

Business colleagues often claim, "With high unemployment, we don't need unions."

I cannot subscribe to this view. The industrialised nations have unionism today because our forefathers cruelly exploited their workers. Today I see people in unions who are not only well educated, but often better qualified than the management with which they must deal. And I have the uneasy feeling that some companies, and certainly some managers, would exploit the workers again if the protection of unions was forfeited.

In 1982 I identified a vulnerable, publicly-listed British publishing company for a company client of mine. We made a bid to secure 27 per cent of this large company. We were challenged by management, but moved swiftly to 100 per cent.

Why was this company unsuccessful? Firstly, its profit had fallen from £1.5 million to £200 000. It had had workers on strike for almost nine months and a management that was strangled by boards at each business level. In fact, all that top management did each day was attend a board meeting somewhere within the company.

The new owners invited me to sort it all out, so the first thing I did as acting chairman was contact the district chief of the journalists' union. I introduced myself and told him frankly that I intended to strip out bad management, trim the workforce, and bring the company back to profitability. Significantly, I would allow the workers greater participation and profit sharing. I felt I could resolve everything without his help, but I wanted the good will of the workers. I told him that he should call me personally if anyone contested my statements.

I then called meetings with the union reps — including the Father of the Chapel (head of the company's union) who was, in fact, a young woman — and the top management with their personnel and specialist advisers.

As I sat through interminable meetings, I observed that the union people were energetic, articulate, visionary and caring. By contrast the management people appeared conservative, boring, rudderless and hopeless.

That afternoon I invited the union people to join me for drinks at the local pub. Management, to this point, had not spoken directly to the workers for nine months, the entire duration of the strike. Management told me that all the workers wanted was their redundancy pay. The union people, after a few drinks and a few tears, had a different view: "We want self-respect and a meaningful job, not a sum of money with no meaning for the future."

I reassured them that they could in future approach me with their problems. Then I sacked the management, from the chairman to the chief executive officer, installed a vigorous young team, and promptly introduced profit sharing. Moreover, I appointed a young woman to the main board. Suddenly this moribund institution was up and running again.

After I had completed my role as temporary chairman/chief executive officer, I returned to the Singapore owners with my recommendations. I said that the company had bought a football team, not a football field, and that human relations and profit sharing were the keys to its future survival. I am pleased to say that twelve months later the company showed a profit of £5.8 million — and we had paid £6 million for the whole company. We had saved this company with simple reorganisation and a sensitivity to human relations. We had listened to the workers.

Sadly, many years later other minds introduced new controls that started to pull apart that successful football team. Why?

Because the people were earning too much money! A bureaucracy of small-minded people from head office swooped in. And the result? They eroded good will and shot millions of pounds down the drain because their quality, visionary people eventually left in disillusionment. (Many of those same people set up their own companies and have been very successful indeed.)

## COMPULSORY UNIONISM

At one stage, the Hamlyn Group had 1000 employees in Australia, none of whom belonged to a union. As far as I knew, the only other company in New South Wales that employed no union staff was Avon Cosmetics. This suited everybody until mid-1975, when the country had a surplus of employment.

The unions decided it was time to move in on us.

What did we do? Well, not that much, because we believed our paternalistic attitude to staff made unionism unnecessary. The following are some of the measures we had taken:

- All offices were carpeted.
- The canteen was cheap and had quality food.
- There was a swimming pool for staff use at lunchtime and on weekends.
- The working environment was surrounded by prize-winning gardens.
- There were profit-sharing schemes.
- There was a bonus scheme.
- There were no bundy clocks in the warehouse.
- Everyone had direct access to the managing director.
- There was flexible time off for the staff for emergencies.

The unions insisted on meeting all staff, which I agreed to with a spirit of friendly co-operation. To help their task, I insisted that all divisional managers meet them to discuss the union problems as a group. Not once did I or any of my team attempt to dissuade staff from joining a union.

After three months they gave up, but not without a threat from one source that they might cripple the company by getting the Transport Workers' Union to stop all the goods coming in and out.

Unbeknown to me at the time, the local Transport Workers' Union representative made an appointment to meet our administration manager, who threw him out.

"He was an Abo from the Transport Workers' Union," I was told later. "I demanded he leave the building immediately."

"You're a fool!" I exploded. "What's his name?" I rang at once and arranged to meet him.

When I met this man to apologise for our outrageous behaviour, I felt a growing admiration for him as we talked. As a boy he had lived in a hut on the outskirts of Taree. Eventually he had become a truck driver, then a union delegate and finally the district representative. He took particular pride in his son, who was about to graduate from university.

His description of the confrontation was withering: "As soon as your man met me, he treated me like dirt. Even before I opened my mouth he abused me." Thankfully we parted with mutual respect.

The last words in our discussions with the union movement were with the head union man.

"I guess all the unions could do for your staff is to get the pool heated," he said.

"It already is," I replied. That head man later became the Premier of New South Wales, Barrie Unsworth.

On the other hand, Avon suffered terrible confrontations with the unions. They had their goods stopped on the wharfs and were forced to unionise staff. Maybe we were just lucky.

## CONSIDER THE UNION VIEWPOINT

Perhaps I found it easy to listen to the union view because I had an empathy with their cause. In my first job as a process engraver, I was a member of the then Printing Trades Union of Australia. As secretary and delegate of the union shop, I achieved a lot at the ripe old age of twenty. Among other things, I founded what was to become one of the biggest swimming clubs in Queensland, the Printing Union Swimming Club.

During this time I developed a lot of respect for the head of the Printing Union, Bert Milliner. Milliner later became a senator in Federal Parliament. His untimely death, during the Whitlam era, presented the opportunity for the Joh Bjelke-Petersen senate manoeuvre that precipitated the downfall of the government and a bitter constitutional crisis.

Bert was a man of the people and a special bloke. (His son is now a minister in the Queensland government.)

## BLACK BANNED

The Hamlyn Group launched a very successful partwork magazine in 1971 called *Australia's Wildlife Heritage*. The advertising and promotion were controversial from the start.

Gough Whitlam had just been elected Prime Minister and we were able to persuade his wife, Margaret, to present our TV commercials. How did we get her? It was simple. We had the gall to ask and she agreed, with the proviso that a fee be donated to various conservation groups around Australia. Thanks to Margaret Whitlam, many groups received typewriters and photocopiers that they wouldn't have done otherwise.

The Prime Minister agreed to launch *Australia's Wildlife Heritage*. After the formalities, a concerned Prime Minister called me aside. "Kevin," he said, "before coming here, I had a call from the Trades and Labour Council. They asked me not to launch your project. It has been printed in Singapore and a lot of Australian printing is going to the East. So the printers' union, in collaboration with the Waterside Workers' Union, is going to black ban you as an example. Your containers on the wharf will not move for months. Do you know anyone in the unions?"

I was horrified! Television promotion was to start the following week, costing $280 000 (about $2 million in today's terms). I could see it all disappearing down the drain. I could hardly believe it.

My first thoughts were wild ones. I would hire a big helicopter and gather a team to snatch the containers off the wharf. I even considered riding in on a big truck, armed with a shotgun, to steal my own books from the wharf. I was desperate.

"I know Senator Milliner. He used to be in the union and so was I," I said.

"Yes, he may help you. All the best, Kevin!" Whitlam replied.

I raced home after the launch and rang an old workmate,

*Prime Minister Gough Whitlam and the author at the launching of*
Australia's Wildflife Heritage *in 1971 — a night remembered for more*
*reasons than one.*

Ken McRae. I told him my problem. He urged me to leave it with
him. At 10 am on that bleak Monday, Bert Milliner, Ken McRae
and the head of the printing union met in my office. Away I went. I
told the union man that I was (and remain so today) one of the
biggest buyers of book printing in Australia. This latest project,
being very sensitive on price and turnaround, simply had to be
printed in Singapore. Furthermore, there was no-one at that time
in Australia who could print the job well enough.

To my utter relief my defence was accepted and the matter
resolved.

I turned to Bert Milliner, "Bert, how can I ever repay you?"

"You don't need to, Kevin," he said. "You did a lot of good things
for me and my members years ago."

The lessons for management are clear. If you treat your
employees with the respect and attention they deserve, your good
faith will be repaid in kind. And if you ever run foul of the unions,
don't hesitate to sit down and explain your situation. In most cases,
a reasonable argument will be heard out.

# CHAPTER 12

# ORGANISATION

Too many managers spend too much time on organisation
and not enough on the real purpose of it all.

**K.E.W.**

The only formal business training available in Australia in the late 1950s was a Certificate and Diploma of Management.

The five-year technical college course coincided with a period when Drucker's Scientific Management was the vogue philosophy worldwide, the thrust of which was that we should develop specialists in industry. The Company Organisational Chart was absolutely essential. So was a Personnel Job Specification and Responsibility List, and a Job Assessment Form.

As a 25-year-old general manager of a small publishing company, I set about the task of plotting all my personnel into these organisational straitjackets with gusto.

As I matured in management, however, I discovered that every time I gave a staff member an organisational chart, showing the neat square where they sat, they would thereafter never shift from that square to help any other square. It wasn't long before that damn organisational chart created bad morale rather than an "A-Team".

Over the past twenty years, while still noting organisational charts for my own use, I have only distributed them to divisional managers and general managers.

## OVER-ORGANISATION

I am always amazed at how over-organised companies, charities, school committees, sporting bodies, defence forces and even the local church group can be. More time is spent on the organisation than the purpose for which the organisation is created. Too many people are employed, too many meetings are held and too many minutes recorded. I call this the "Who-broke-the-window-in-the-toilet?" syndrome.

As a young man I was president of a Queensland surf club. When I was transferred to Sydney in my job, I was asked to attend my last club committee meeting, after which there would be a farewell drink. The meeting went on till 12.30 am. You might have expected the meeting to discuss the recruitment of new members to patrol the beaches in an effort to reduce drownings. But no! The evening was spent on the right to vote, on the rules of the club, but mostly on the question of "Who broke the window in the toilet?"

When I became president of the World Lifesaving movement in 1971, I was invited to attend a celebration at my old club — once again after the club committee meeting. By now the club had a major problem with membership and beach patrols, but they were still wrestling with the challenge of yet another broken window. I could no longer contain myself.

"Fellows, who cares about the broken window? Our energies should be spent on training members in efficient methods of lifesaving and in preventing drowning on our beaches. The toilet window problem should be dispensed with quickly and the evening devoted to major problems!"

I guarantee that at this moment — even as you read — boards around the world are locked in debate over "Who-broke-the-toilet-window?", instead of asking, "What are we *really* here for?"

The following articles appeared in the same issue of the *International Herald Tribune,* Paris edition, August 1992.

### GENERAL MOTORS IMPROVES BUT STILL REMAINS IN THE RED

*From our correspondent in New York*

General Motors, the world's largest car maker and owner of Vauxhall and Opel, remained in the red in the second quarter of this year, but put in its best quarterly performance since 1991.

Depressing profits was a $749 million special charge to pay for 9000 job cuts at its electronics division that pushed second quarter losses to $357 million, against a loss of $784 million for the same period a year ago.

Without that special charge GM continued in the black with a $392 million profit, up from an $808 million loss last year and double the profits made in the first half. But Mr Robert Stempel, GM's chairman, said: "Sustaining the rate of progress we experienced in the first half of this year, however, appears to be extremely challenging." He said the second half of the year could prove difficult in view of uncertainties related to the pace of the Northern American economic recovery and a slow-down in some key European markets.

Last year GM lost almost $10 billion on its American car operations, but has seen a 5 per cent rise in American vehicle sales and a 1 per cent increase in second quarter market share to 36.9 per cent. Worldwide car and truck sales climbed 6 per cent to just over two million but overseas car and truck sales fell 3 per cent to 670 500.

Without special redundancy charges, profits for the half year came out at $572 million against a $218 million loss on total revenue, 11 per cent higher at $67.2 billion. The electronic division's special charge pushed GM into the red by $217 million compared with half-time losses of $928 million last year.

But the figures disappointed Wall Street, which marked GM's shares down 75 cents to $38.375 after executives indicated there would be no further plant closures this year.

Jack Kirnan, Salomon Bros' automotive analyst, downgraded his outlook on GM and cut his 1992 estimates to break even from a previous estimated profit of $1.25 a share. Mr Kirnan also cut his 1993 estimate on GM to a profit of $3.50 a share from a previous estimate of about $5 a share. "Softer European sales could exacerbate GM's problems in North America," Mr Kirnan said.

## IBM SET TO ANNOUNCE $7BN PC DIVISION

*From our correspondent in New York*

International Business Machines (IBM) is believed to be set to announce the formation of a new personal computer division, which would have sales of $7 billion and rank as the world's largest.

The move would be the first tangible evidence of IBM's strategy to form itself into six smaller parts that could respond much more rapidly to changes in the market place.

Shares of IBM, whose chairman is John Akers, were down again yesterday at $90, off more than $4 in two days after executives forecast little or no growth this year in its core business, mainframe computers.

One analyst cut his forecast of IBM's full year profit figures by 15 per cent. IBM will cut at least 32 000 staff this year, bringing total dismissed since 1986 to 92 000. A separate PC division would streamline all business functions under one group. Its personal computers are currently developed and made by IBM, but marketing decisions and distribution are handled by a separate part of IBM.

The company will not comment on the plan, but industry sources say James Cannavino, head of personal systems, got the go-ahead to reform the division some time ago and is expected to disclose details within the next two weeks. Analysts are uncertain just what profit prospects would be for a separate PC division amid the most fierce price war in PC history.

It is understood that IBM has plans to float shares of the division on Wall Street after three years.

Fresh doubts over the company's profit prospects emerged last month despite a surge in earnings for April, May and June from $126 million to $714 million. Gross profits from its hardware sales, which account for half IBM's revenue, actually fell and the company said job cuts would cost it a further $1.2 billion.

The reports on two of the largest corporations in the world showed one still adhering to what Toffler calls the "smokestack" mentality of "bigger is better", and the other determined to be broken into smaller, flexible businesses to compete more adequately with its opposition around the world.

## THE COMPANY MANUAL

Company manuals are produced in vast numbers by most of the world's major corporations. They may be thicker than the Bible but they're nowhere near as good to read. (Come to think of it, all the guidance you will ever need in business, you can find in the Bible. Did not Jesus surround himself with twelve great divisional managers? Didn't they believe they had a great product to sell? And didn't they function with a small, simple organisation? Within ten years the then known world knew about their product. Many millions bought it and set up franchise offices, and it survives today. The only problems they ever really had with their product over the centuries arose when they drifted into the area of over-documentation, producing esoteric but confusing manuals. In short, they stopped communicating with their real market, the common man. What the twelve lads had set out to do was ruined by a growing bureaucracy.)

I venture to suggest that if you collected 1000 company manuals, barely 10 per cent would succeed in imparting knowledge, providing guidance or inspiring the reader. It is a moot point whether they would even be comprehensible.

Certainly none would ever be enthralling or uplifting enough to move staff to clutch it to their breasts, cry "My God, I belong!", and dash down the street to tell the world about it.

## THE MANUAL MUST BE TOP SECRET

A big mistake many companies make in producing a Corporate Policy and Operations Manual is that they reveal the most confidential details of their management methods, marketing techniques, production secrets and, more importantly, future strategies.

I have been horrified to have manuals from opposition companies plonked on my desk by personnel who thought it would get them a job. Regardless of the questionable ethics of accepting such "gifts", it would only have been a matter of time before such people did the same to me.

In fact, I rest comfortably in the knowledge that no person employed by me in the last twenty-five years has ever divulged the secrets of *our* Corporate Policy and Operations Manuals. Why? Because I have never had one!

I confess to having tried to create one from time to time, but they always ended up being as academic, boring and inflexible as any others. Today, more than ever, companies that cannot move fast and remain innovative will not stay successful for long. For any manual to be useful in this frenetic climate it would have to be very, very flexible indeed.

It will be obvious to readers that I have avoided the conservative path in management. I was often told my methods did not conform with company policy before being handed a 60 mm-thick Operations Manual. Hours of searching would fail to reveal the policy I'd broken because, in the end, what passes for company policy tends to rest only in the mind of your superior — and they interpret it to suit themselves.

In 1964, I read a Modern Library copy of Machiavelli's *The Prince and the Discourses*. Later, because I sold that list in Australia, I re-read it — and the penny dropped. Here was the most perfect Policy and Operations Manual ever written. It may have been written in the sixteenth century, but if you change the "King" to the "Chief Executive Officer" and all the other characters into managers, advisers and the like, it is all there. I used to recommend the book to all my managers. Someone else had the same idea in the mid-1970s, because at that time Penguin published *Machiavelli and Management*.

I once employed two managers from the same family. Unfortunately, I cut back the activities of one and finally terminated our relationship. But I kept the other brother on. I was never quite forgiven for this and when the employed brother was ready he left abruptly, to our great inconvenience. Machiavelli would have expected it. He wrote: "The prince must never execute a close adviser and keep the adviser's brother as a bodyguard or one day the brother will do the prince harm in revenge."

# CHAPTER 13

# "MY GOD, IT'S A WOMAN!"

I have more female than male friends in business and,
in Weldon International, nearly 90 per cent of my total staff
and more than 60 per cent of my managers are women.

**K.E.W.**

Women have played a big part in any success I have achieved in life, particularly in business. I have more female than male friends in business and, in Weldon International, nearly 90 per cent of my total staff and more than 60 per cent of my managers are women. True, my industry attracts an unusually large number of women, but not in these proportions.

Why do I choose to employ so many women? Allow me to explain my attitude obliquely. I have been involved in aviation for many years, piloting my own aircraft since the early 1970s. It's a pursuit that is inclined to be elitist, with some flyers believing themselves to be much cleverer than those who don't fly. They are not. Any good instructor will tell you that if you can drive a car, you can fly a plane. Another misconception is that aviation is only for clever males. Passengers are still shocked when they discover that the pilot of their huge jet is a woman. Yet women have played a significant role in world aviation, not least Australian women.

As early as 1912, a gorgeous country girl called Harriet Quimby became America's first woman pilot. She flew a Bleriot across the English Channel to France. Even then her achievement was not appropriately fêted — the sinking of the Titanic stole her headlines! She was followed by a long line of women pilots more familiar to us, such as Amy Johnson and Amelia Earhart.

*Nancy Bird-Walton, pictured with the author during an air race in the UK, flew an aerial ambulance in the outback during the 1930s. The author borrowed the title of her book for this chapter heading.*

## Australian women pilots

During the 1930s, Nancy Bird-Walton flew an aerial ambulance in outback Australia. The response to her first job summed up the attitude of many men to women in aviation (and business!) and provided the title for her recently completed biography. Ringing a property owner to explain she was the pilot picking up the patient, she overheard him exclaim to his mate, "My God, it's a woman!" It didn't seem to hinder *her* career.

Nor those who followed in her footsteps. I recently flew my Tiger Moth to a gathering of de Havilland aircraft at Woburn Abbey in the UK. As I stood chatting to a few people I noticed a very frail lady patiently waiting to talk to me. Her name was Dr Hamilton and she introduced herself as a "dinkum Aussie".

"I'm from Adelaide and it's wonderful to see you Australians here," she enthused. "I've just flown 109 miles myself in that old 1930s Hornet Moth over there. I'll be popping off to fly home again to get my husband's dinner. He's frail, you see, at eighty-three. I'm flying back tomorrow for another day and I'll fly back again Sunday afternoon." She was seventy-nine years old.

A few years ago a mother of small children, convinced she was just an ordinary housewife, decided she would prove otherwise by being the first Australian woman to fly solo around the world. She flew across great oceans with minimal aviation gear, at one time flying within a few feet of raging seas trying to fix her auxiliary fuel pump. Gaby Kennard arrived back in Australia having achieved the nigh-impossible.

What more can I say of women and achievement? And I've only covered the narrow field of aviation.

## I OWE THEM

Before paying homage to some of the successful female executives I have appointed or done business with, I must acknowledge the profound influence my secretaries have had on my career. They have at various times been my guides, my critics, my ears and my eyes. The title, "secretary", scarcely does justice to the significance of their roles.

When I was about twenty-four and working for the Grenville group I was awarded my first secretary, a married woman of twenty-six. I'd never so much as written a formal business letter in my life, let alone dictated one.

"Mrs Moss," I said authoritatively, "take this letter." Halfway through Mrs Moss looked up at me and shook her head.

"It's terrible," she said.

"You really think so?" I said, somewhat deflated.

"Oh, yes," she said, "but might I suggest ..."

That was just the beginning of women helping me along the path. After Mrs Moss, there was Jenny Rudwick, a twenty-one-year-old who added a little softness to the office atmosphere. Autocratic and ever-eager, I would constantly call, "Jenny come and take this letter! ... Jenny get me the file!" This behaviour so upset Pam Seaborn, the very efficient secretary in the next office, that she told Jenny, "I wouldn't work for that so-and-so, the way he yells! Thank heavens *my* boss is a gentle soul with impeccable manners."

When I left the Grenville group, I left a very special secretary in Jenny Rudwick. My next secretary was Bernadette Giles, who was different again. She joined as my first staff member when I was starting up a new company (Paul Hamlyn Pty Ltd). She was involved in organising the building of our offices and employing the first staff. She had enormous energy and enthusiasm, but after the madness of establishing the company, Bernadette was determined to see the world.

Now Bernadette, Jenny Rudwick and Pam Seaborn used to meet regularly. My idiosyncrasies, it seems, were frequently a topic of conversation. Thankfully, it didn't prevent Bernadette suggesting I consider Pam to replace her.

I had always been impressed by Pam's speed and efficiency, so I had no hesitation in hiring her. Twenty-one years later we still maintain a close association and, I'm happy to report, I have learned something about shouting along the way. A compassionate woman who always has the welfare of the company at heart, Pam possesses a talent for discreetly communicating staff problems to management and management problems to staff. Unfailingly loyal to those loyal to her, Pam will keep a secret like no-one I know. It is no surprise that my top business associates respect Pam as much as I do and, with my urging, she has gone on to establish her own business, Pam Seaborn and Associates. She handles many outside companies' special events and public relations, as well as any events among our own companies that we feel need her special touch.

## OTHER SUCCESSFUL WOMEN

I'm sure my one-time chief Paul Hamlyn would concede that he owes some of his success in establishing Octopus Books to his (then) startling appointment of a woman, Sue Thompson, as his managing director. She was outstanding in the management role, coming from the IPC Hamlyn Group, London. She was also a great negotiator, organiser and planner. Paul Hamlyn made her a very successful managing director, a shareholder and subsequently a multi-millionaire. My view was that if it was good enough for Paul to have female managers, I certainly wasn't going to be backward in doing the same.

When I took over the Marshall Cavendish Group in London, I immediately appointed a very talented editorial woman, Liz Glaze, as a director. My confidence was justified. She went on to be very successful, establishing her own magazine, *Essentials*, and, to this day, she has lost none of her wonderful enthusiasm.

## THE MALE ATTITUDE

Women are still often disadvantaged when a male has to choose between a woman and a man for a management position. Why? I believe it is because men feel less threatened by their own, familiar gender.

I urge men to pay attention to the many successful women in business and note their performance. They will be surprised.

I also urge women to resist the temptation to disguise their physical differences in the belief that they need to do so to compete successfully. To my mind they are taking a step backward by dressing in severe, businesslike gear, or "power dressing" as it is called. In their tailored jackets and business skirts they are starting to look like their male counterparts in boring, conservative business suits. All much the same and colourless. Successful businesswomen should challenge the stereotype by wearing colourful, fashionable clothes. Looking glamorous certainly doesn't suggest that they are any less articulate, intelligent or capable.

Thank God for women in business, I say. But stay that way.

# CHAPTER 14

# THE COMPANY CAR

The company car is so ingrained in the Australian
business culture that many seek a transfer
for this incentive alone.

**K.E.W.**

The company car, viewed in Australia as much as a right as a privilege, is a continuing source of friction between management and staff. It represents a huge cost that has to be borne by all segments of industry.

Australian businesses, unlike their counterparts in most other countries, usually make company cars available for middle and supervising management. In most cases, it is interpreted as an add-on benefit rather than an integral part of a salary or wage package. The company car is so ingrained in Australian business culture that many seek a transfer for this incentive alone; some will even move to a different industry in order to claim this perk. After so long as an intrinsic part of the Australian business scene, it is difficult to see how expectations can be altered.

The company car has been described as the car that, "never needs washing, polishing or vacuuming; never needs an oil change or service; and needs little petrol during the week but lots on weekends." A joke? I hope so!

Deciding who should be entitled to which company car requires keen judgement. Be cautious — the path of good intentions is a minefield for senior management. Here are some of the "special requests" I have fielded over the years.

I would really like this second-hand Jaguar as my company car. If the company pays me the equivalent of the company Holden Commodore, I will put in the difference.

Really? What about the repair bills, petrol consumption, and so on?

> I've just had twins, and with the other three kids I need a station wagon. The company can use it when it's needed.

This request was granted, but he neglected to mention that the station wagon was a four-wheel drive with specially fitted springs, a spotlight on the roof and wide gorilla tyres. And he wouldn't let the warehouse near it when they wanted to use it to load some cartons. The only thing that saved him and the car was the size of the orders he landed.

## COMPANY CAR CAPERS

### The "Claytons" company car
This was the car that only pretended to be a company vehicle. The manager who had it commuted each day by ferry. But then again, his wife *did* drive him to and from the ferry in it!

### The company car with the long-range tank
It never ceased to amaze me how a company car could be brim full of petrol late Friday and bone dry on Monday. Even more staggering, the tank could be full late one afternoon during the week, yet empty the next morning. Hmmm!

### The company car accident
These are enormously costly overheads for a company. Experience teaches me that 90 per cent could be avoided. We once had such a huge run of prangs in a fleet of ninety-five company cars that I insisted all drivers provide written details of the accidents to me as managing director. This alone reduced the number of accidents over a twelve-month period. Among my favourite explanations tendered were:

- Brushing off a hot cigarette ash from the lap while driving.
- Watching a good-looking girl on the footpath and thumping into the car ahead!

## Special-purpose company cars

This is the car that has to be custom-made to be a walk-in workshop, photographic laboratory, caravan, or mini-bus capable of touring anywhere in Australia, including mountains as high as Mt Kosciusko and salt lakes as vast as Lake Eyre. When the person it was built for leaves, just try to sell it!

Then there was the car that had pure leather reclining seats, press-button windows, sunroof, racing trim tyres, iridescent enamelled finish, fog-lights (for Australia?), Gucci ski racks and, wait for it, a leather-bound copy of *Gregory's Street Directory*. All this was supposedly to impress VIPs when they were collected from the airport. Regrettably the man who used it was never in the country when a VIP arrived!

## Cleanliness is next to godliness

Senior managers who call a snap inspection of their cars are invariably in for a shock. They find that company cars seldom receive oil checks or proper maintenance, and are even less frequently washed and polished.

I recall borrowing the car of one of my managers, a keen environmentalist. When I leaped into his car — The Company Car! — it was littered with empty drink bottles, potato crisp packets, old newspapers and the like. When I told him the car was filthy, he said, "Better to throw it in the car than pollute the streets!"

## The takeover and the "new car policy"

I know of several cases where the model of company car has influenced multi-million dollar acquisitions. People in the takeover company always seem to assume that the people they have taken over should immediately be slotted into *their* company car policy.

For example, one of the largest international public companies in food processing and distribution took over a meat export and processing business in the 1970s. It was attracted to the meat company because of its great success in marketing and customer service and the entrepreneurial skills of the chief executive, a man young enough to make the company he had sold even more successful. No sooner had the ink dried on the deal than the young executive was set upon by some group personnel martinet. The executive was informed that the subsidiary company management cars had to be Ford Fairlanes, certainly not the Jaguar he had been driving for years.

The entrepreneur's immediate reaction was that any new owner prepared to reduce his status didn't really want him in the long term. "To hell with it, I'll buy my own Jaguar!" he told the martinet. To his surprise, the new chief executive didn't help. "Well, it *is* company policy," he said, thus sowing the seed which ultimately led to the talented young executive's departure. There followed a rapid deterioration of the company, and when the dust settled it had cost the takeover company $16 million — all for the difference between a Ford Fairlane and a Jaguar. Absurd!

In my experience the car arrangements should be left as they are in any takeover. Don't try to fit the architects of exciting companies into the little boxes that big organisations like to impose!

When I founded the Hamlyn Group in Australia, our parent company was the International Publishing Corporation (IPC). It had a few other existing activities in Australia, including the English publishing company Odhams, which was run very successfully by Robert Hill, a wonderful English gentleman much respected in the publishing industry. When I made him Melbourne manager of our expanded group I was immediately confronted with the car problem. Robert's chosen car was a large Chevrolet, which he would buy second-hand and would cost a little more than the normal new Holden. A fellow in London picked this up and, reminding me of the international group policy, told me to get him into the standard Holden.

This is how I read the situation. Here was a man who felt good about the car he had driven into his driveway for years. Now his neighbours would wonder why he had been demoted. I allowed Robert to keep his car. Indeed, two years later he renewed it with another second-hand Chev.

Just before his retirement dinner, I discovered we'd written off his Chev and all we had in our asset register was "car air-conditioner". So I took some pleasure in a retirement present — on behalf of the group —of a new air-conditioner wrapped up in an eight-year-old Chevrolet Impala! At least *that* car drama ended happily.

When the Paul Hamlyn Group Australia became a subsidiary of Reed Consolidated Industries, I was informed by the chief executive of Reed that my Jaguar exceeded "the Reed car policy". Would I adjust to a Volvo forthwith? I refused because my car standard had been in my original contract. (In fact, I reminded the person concerned that the man who ran a subsidiary budget music division I had acquired two years earlier also drove a Jaguar — the standard he had been used to. This executive had doubled the profits of the group since the takeover, largely because we left him alone.) I concluded my argument by suggesting that if any of the parent company's other directors preferred a Jaguar, then obviously they should join the Hamlyn Group!

## CHAPTER 15

# COPING WITH BAD PRESS

*The prospect of bad publicity should always be reported
to the chief executive, who must then take control.*

**K.E.W.**

Management tends to be too cavalier about bad publicity. Yet it happens to all of us sooner or later, particularly to those companies with a large number of people in the front line.

A customer returning a faulty product is told, "Sorry, we can't replace it." The next thing we know, some consumer affairs body homes in and management is wriggling on the hook trying to prove its innocence.

Too often I've seen bad publicity poorly handled by personnel or public relations officers, particularly on television or radio. Because they are unsure of themselves in the glare of the spotlight, they appear devious or dishonest. Viewers or listeners immediately side with the victim, regardless of the facts. Untold damage can be done to a company this way.

An example of this was an interview with a bank representative following the bankruptcy of the popular Leyland Brothers. Mike and Mal had run short of funds attempting to develop a theme park in New South Wales. Obviously they hadn't adequately planned their investment and had been obliged to keep increasing their very high borrowings. Like many others, they were required to put up personal guarantees. Eventually their bank, which had a proper business contract, called in the personal guarantees. It was sad to see the Leyland family trapped in such debt, but we all have to face the consequences of our financial obligations if we miscalculate. Anyway, the Commonwealth Bank's spokesman, obviously nervous in front of the media, did his best to explain the situation. But the bank came out looking like the villain again. I felt the situation needed more of a hands-on manager to explain the unfortunate outcome forthrightly. The appropriate spokesperson would have clearly reiterated the various stages of the arrangement between the bank and the Leylands before the day of reckoning. Sure, it wasn't as bad for the bank as it might have been, but because banks suffered a bashing by the community in the early 1990s, this publicity certainly didn't help.

Bad publicity takes other forms. Sometimes it can be inadvertently promoted by the institutions themselves. Take banks again. There is a decades-old public perception that big banks pretend to be what they are not. Misleading image-building is the charge. Remember the ads about how friendly the Commonwealth Bank manager was, the man who would do absolutely *anything* for you? Of course no bank can afford to be that generous, and the viewers knew it. It was just an image dreamed up for promotion which, because of its patent absurdity, ultimately did more harm than good.

A former boss of mine, Keith Davenport, once told me of an abortive promotion by the Reed Group, which at the time was racked with industrial stoppages and poor productivity. The public relations personnel manager at head office gathered all personnel managers together and announced a whole new international image. Standing before huge banners proclaiming "Reed is People", he harangued the miserable souls huddled in front of him. "Reed is People!" he repeated grandly. "Reed is People!" A small Celtic gentleman at the back of the hall could contain himself no longer.

"Rubbish! Rubbish!" bellowed the man.

This personnel manager had the courage to challenge the head office's blustery promotional thrust, a thrust which flew in the face of overwhelming evidence that Reed (at the time) didn't really give a stuff about people. His clear-sightedness enabled the campaign to be killed and a new direction taken.

## THE MEDIA

The media usually approaches complaints about a company fairly, creating a balanced report that gives the company involved a proper chance to clear its name. When wayward businesses or managers are confronted and, it is hoped, weeded out, I am as delighted as the next man.

From time to time, however, the media will make a wickedly biased attack, weighting the air time so that the company representative's reply or explanation is edited to suit the overall objective of the producer. I have seen such reporting send quite innocent companies to the wall, throwing families out of work and crucifying an individual who has spent a lifetime's energies and savings building a company. This is unforgivable.

To sum up, the prospect of bad publicity should always be reported to the chief executive, who must then take control. If matters of this nature are not handled correctly, they can push the most innocent business to the edge of disaster.

CHAPTER 16

# THE FRONT LINE

What exactly do we mean when we say
"good morning" or "good afternoon"?

K.E.W.

The "front door" of a company can be the first person who answers the phone, or the receptionist who greets people in the foyer. In hotels, it can be the registration clerk, the doorman, or the person in charge of the breakfast room.

A friend once told me a story about a New York City hotel that had just been built for $30 million, then a substantial investment. When it opened, the hotel had an excellent 80 per cent occupancy.

After six months, occupancy suddenly declined to 70 per cent. Then 50 per cent. The owners called in all the experts, altered their promotion and offered discounts, but the decline continued.

Then they called in a trusty old hotel consultant who did nothing but check into the hotel as a guest to scrutinise the staff and the service. He then interviewed past guests. The answer became very clear to him.

"It's the grumpy old bitch in charge of the breakfast room," he reported. The woman in question shouted at the guests and made them line up and wait. Because she was unhappy, all her staff were unhappy. The atmosphere was terrible and the guests felt it.

One person at the company front door had jeopardised a huge investment.

How often have we entered an office to find no-one at reception, or someone so impolite that you feel you are imposing on their time? A reception area should always be neat, with fresh flowers and a well-presented, friendly person in attendance to greet visitors

— certainly not someone looking bored, or reading a paperback. Seats should be comfortable and handy reading matter should provide a background to the company, with illustrations showing the company's product. Use the time spent by visitors in reception as an opportunity to promote the company's interest.

Most of all, don't keep people waiting in reception. If you can't avoid it, send someone to keep them company. It is plain rude to keep people waiting without explanation, particularly when they have made an appointment.

## THE SWITCHBOARD

Why are most companies so slack about their switchboards? Why does the phone ring for so long? Why are you assured you won't be kept waiting (you already have, of course) before you get switched to Muzak to wait? And wait. And why, when the phone is answered promptly, should the voice sound bored, unfriendly or abrupt? Your first reaction is to wonder what the devil the rest of the company is going to be like.

How often have we been kept waiting when trying to book an airline flight, or order a refrigerator from a retail outlet? We may well ask why the company advertises in the Yellow Pages if it can't answer our call and handle enquiries promptly.

For those companies without a central switchboard, whoever answers should be as efficient and friendly as a good switchboard operator.

These are some of the things a good switch *won't* say:

- "Good morning," when it's "Good afternoon."
- "Sorry, Mr Jones is still at lunch," when it's four in the afternoon.
- "Mr Jones is still in a meeting," when it's been the only response to this particular enquirer for the past two weeks.
- "He hasn't arrived yet," and it's eleven o'clock in the morning.
- "I'm sorry, he's still on holidays." And has been for six weeks.
- "No, you can't speak to the managing director, he no longer works here." This may be a particular problem when the caller happens to be the manager of the company's bank.

- "Just a moment, I'll put you on hold." Five minutes later the caller is forgotten, along with the reason he or she called.

Other switchboard *faux pas* are:
- The airline you call gives you five minutes of the company's flight discount promotions before you can utter a word.
- You are pleasantly surprised when the switch puts you through quickly, until you discover the party you seek is on long service leave and won't be back for two more months. Why didn't the switch know?
- Returning a call, you ask what the company does, and they reply, "Don't know, I just work the switch."
- Having to repeat or spell your name many times. A particularly uncomfortable example I recall featured a Mr Crunt. Then there was the eminent chemist from La Roche in Switzerland, on tour with the Australian subsidiary, who had no end of trouble when she called. Her name was Miss Schitz.
- The switch operator with slow speech when you're in a hurry or, even worse, the American gush: "Good morning. Welcome to America's leading toothpaste corporation. This is Marybell speaking and I'm here to help you. Would you mind holding on for just a few moments and ... you have a nice day, do you hear?" The only thing she didn't mention was that you would "hold" for half an hour.

Everyone in business is responsible for the standards we live with. If you are kept waiting in reception a long time without attention, complain. If the phone takes a long time to answer, say so. Help lift the standard by not accepting poor service. Not only will you be doing yourself a favour, but in the end you will be helping the company you are complaining about.

After all, what exactly do we mean by "good morning" or "good afternoon"?

## THE FACSIMILE MACHINE

Another front door to your company is the fax — often the first contact these days. Therefore it is obvious that a fax document should be clearly identified, and the content precise and friendly.

The peremptory style of some faxes does nothing to promote a friendly relationship, and business can be lost forever because of poor, or unnecessarily blunt, communication. Writing letters and faxes is of the utmost importance, but be friendly when you do so.

# CHAPTER 17

# THE COURAGE TO DREAM

Ambitious dreams, boldly realised, can set standards
that influence others long after we've gone.

**K.E.W.**

Everyone should have a "dream of dreams", however bold or humble. Most business people, if honest with themselves, would admit that they have spent quiet moments dreaming of achieving apparently impossible goals, the "dream of dreams". I believe this sort of fantasy is healthy. In fact, I always ask those who work closely with me about their dream of dreams. It helps them identify what really motivates them, what their long-term aspirations might be, even though they may change. I have also found it helpful for slotting people into the right role.

This question so fascinates me that whenever I have been with one of the great achievers in life, I've asked, "Did you ever dream as a kid or as a young adult that you would be the world's leading aviator/astronaut/tennis player/business leader?" Without exception, they had.

Sometimes we review our dream because we are influenced by role models or mentors. Such people can help focus our dream of dreams. Indeed, ambitious dreams, boldly realised, can set standards that influence others long after we've gone.

When I was a young officer at Jervis Bay Naval Depot, I remember discussing how impressed I was with Captain Cook's legacy. His feats of great navigation inspired many of his crew, one of the most celebrated of whom was Lieutenant Bligh.

As Captain Bligh he established himself as a worthy successor when he was forced, after the mutiny on 'The Bounty', to make his monumental voyage of thousands of sea miles to Timor in an open

*The author (left) as a young lieutenant with fellow officers in
the Royal Australian Navy (Res.).*

boat with precious little navigation equipment. Cook also had a
first lieutenant called Matthew Flinders. Flinders went on to etch
his name on the roll of great navigators by circumnavigating
Australia and drafting charts that are still in use today.

The most brilliant navigation in the Americas was that of
Commander George Vancouver, rowing along the freezing land
masses of British Columbia to Alaska in a long boat. He, too, had
served with Cook. Whenever I examined the writings of these men,
a shared vision and resolve came through. Surely this was inspired
to some degree by the role model of Cook, though each
accomplished his own "dream of dreams".

Cook is but one example. After the great Jesse Owens returned
in triumph to America with three gold medals won at the 1936
Berlin Olympics, he gave talks to youngsters around the country,
particularly in the black communities. Among his adoring fans was
a white boy who was so motivated that he too began to dream the
"dream of dreams". "One day I will be a famous runner like

Jesse Owens," said Bob Morrow. Morrow went on to win three gold medals at the Melbourne Olympics twenty years later. He in turn did a similar tour circuit, perhaps infusing another boy with a "dream of dreams". And so it goes on. Certainly Jesse Owens has motivated generations of athletes to dream their "dream of dreams".

## DREAMERS IN BUSINESS

I place business leaders in two categories. The first achieves leadership through plodding dedication and attrition. They take over what exists, add what is recommended, and generally run the business as a manager. Then there's the other type of business leader who, while on their way up, sat in the wings muttering to themselves: "I know what I'd do if I was running this company ..." They nurture their private "dream of dreams".

In my opinion, if the opportunity is presented to this second type, they show themselves to be more rounded, more human, and more able to communicate to all levels of the business. They know where they are going because they are following a vision, whereas the other type of manager's horizons tend to be limited to the corporate plan or the direction of the board.

No matter at what level they function, everyone should be encouraged to have a "dream of dreams". If you can identify your unique dream you will forge ahead. Just try it. Sit down with one of your workers and ask, "What is *your* dream of dreams?" You'll be surprised at the result.

# CHAPTER 18

# CHOOSING THE RIGHT GEAR

*The development of small, cheap, "user-friendly"
personal computers showed many of us ordinary mortals
that computers needn't be mysterious.*

**K.E.W.**

As I write this book, we are at the beginning of a technological surge that will influence business beyond the year 2000. Technology is developing at such a pace that only businesses organised into small units will be flexible enough to exploit it. As Toffler says, any business that clings to the smokestack mentality — believing that massive corporations have the weight to win through — will be left behind.

Technology is now driven more by market forces than by remote research establishments. This has pushed manufacturers to produce smaller and more readily understood electronic machinery in an effort to find sufficient outlets for profitable mass production. In short, complex electronic machinery has become more "user-friendly", that brilliant term coined by the Americans to describe the new wave of computers. A great deal of credit for this approach must be given to the creators of Apple computers. Prior to their arrival on the scene, computer technology was almost exclusively the realm of the scientist or the highly-trained expert. Computer people communicated in the gobbledygook language of computer science, severely limiting a broader use of the technology.

The development of small, cheap, user-friendly personal computers showed many of us ordinary mortals that computers needn't be mysterious. Indeed, being "user friendly" is a guiding principle that should be applied to all business aids.

The fax and personal computer now make it possible to break down monolithic bureaucracies into small units. Everyone should read Toffler's *Power Shift* on the subject. He has been absolutely correct so far about the push towards smaller business.

## The personal computer

The Nippon Insurance Company (NIC) spent $500 million equipping down-the-line insurance people with their own personal computers. It was money well spent as far as I'm concerned, creating a more personal touch by adding speed and flexibility to better serve the needs of the customer. In contrast, insurance companies in the Western world, particularly in Australia, are huge and bureaucratic. Try estimating how long it takes to get a claim processed or a new insurance policy issued. Against such cumbersome methods, I predict that NIC's innovative move will help the Japanese take on the international insurance companies in the next decade. The others will get slower and less efficient while the Japanese, bolstered by their large domestic market, will be well placed to compete internationally. Simply because they have identified the right gear and use it in small units.

New technology mightn't have markedly increased business productivity over the past decade, but I still believe companies without the right gear will get left behind. Convenience and quick access to information cannot be ignored in the equation.

For instance, the simple Apple Macintosh Powerbook I am using as I write has infinitely more versatility than the huge ICL computer I had installed for the Hamlyn Group in 1968. Why wouldn't you have one of these little beauties?

Our own top international sales people and managers travel the world with laptops that have all the company's publishing information programmed in — titles, page content, colour, print runs, prices, and so on. It is commonplace for a customer to want a variation in publishing and the laptop gives us the facility to provide quick answers by pressing a few buttons. That way we can close the deal on the spot. Any agreement can be printed out by simply plugging the laptop into a printer.

In one of our offices in America, we had a couple of laser

printers installed that cost us $10 000 each. Only six months later we didn't hesitate to buy a much faster one with even better resolution costing only $5000. Boy, are we in a revolution!

## THE CAPITAL EXPENDITURE SYNDROME

Businesses around the world are still strangled by inflexible limits on capital expenditure. Managers may be allowed to spend millions on inventory, on raw materials, on creating a line of credits to the customer or on committing the company in areas such as debtors — all of which could send the company broke — but when it comes to equipment, well, that's a *capital* item. And that expenditure level is usually governed by the board.

Some Australian companies owned by British or American parents cannot buy a personal computer unless it is approved by some clerk in London or New York. Why? Because that old system called "capital expenditure" places arbitrary annual limits on such expenditure. Frustrated supervisors and staff generally resent jumping through silly hoops for genuinely-needed new equipment, so they plod along with the old gear.

I know this, because one of our companies in America is so fast and flexible that it can produce a top-quality range of books in six months. Its largest local competitor can take eighteen months to two years to complete a similar series. We leave them for dead because we are small and flexible and have the right gear. We have, however, a long, long way to go in some divisions. The old capital expenditure bogey is hard to shake from people's minds. I have seen very few losses through capital expenditure in my career but, oh boy, have I seen millions poured down the drain in working capital, inventories, debtors and work in progress!

## TECHNOLOGY IS SO SMALL

There is no disputing that the portability and increasing capabilities of new technology offer unimagined advantages. Consider one vital piece of aeronautical equipment, the GPS, or satellite positioning system. It is a tiny machine with a few buttons, about 150mm x 40mm x 150mm deep. I have one in my twin-engine aircraft, coupled with other navigational aids and an

*Flying my vintage Tiger Moth is a stimulating mixture of seat-of-the-pants flying and use of the latest in navigational technology.*

autopilot. I have another in a small pouch in my fifty-year-old Tiger Moth plane. It can fix your position by latitude and longitude anywhere in the world by receiving signals beamed from satellites circling the globe. This little machine monitors the wind aloft and its direction; it tells me what course to steer; it will adjust for the wind, whether head or tail; and it gives me my ground speed. It will also tell me how many miles to the next destination, how to steer there, how long it will take me, and an estimated time of arrival — and more information as I need it. This tiny unit could almost replace the massive panels of instruments you see in big aircraft. It hasn't yet been approved by the CAA, but it will be. By that time the units will be even smaller. This piece of equipment, costing a few thousand dollars, will replace technology that offers half the efficiency and costs $45 000 more.

Already we have computers and communication systems that act upon voice instruction. Small, portable telephones function from ever more remote places and can be carried for use in some of the major Western countries with a small chip adjustment. We can sit in our cars in traffic and talk at great length with a customer in New York City. A few years ago we negotiated one of the biggest business deals of my career between England, the USA and ourselves. It was completed by my divisional chief executives, who spoke on a portable telephone and communicated with a portable fax, all aboard a yacht moored at the Gold Coast's Southport Harbour.

Having praised the new technology, I caution that it is no cure-all. It can help you conduct your business if properly used, but if your organisation is untidy it is just as likely to get you in a bigger mess.

## NEGATIVES OF THE RIGHT GEAR

As previously mentioned, a big problem with instant communication is that people pass information upwards instead of making decisions at the lower levels. The new gear can also create wasteful paperwork and frivolous communication because people don't feel the need to use it sparingly. This can be expensive.

Having said that, if the right gear can perform a job better for your company, go for it. Management that doesn't buy the right gear at the right time is compromising its business.

# CHAPTER 19

# CAN BUSINESS HAVE A HEART?

*You wouldn't have a rum on board, would you?*

AN INNOCENT ABROAD

You will have more fun in business if you regard your business associates as friends. Many business people I've known have said, on retirement, that they got more fulfilment from the special relationships they built up with their co-workers, suppliers and customers than anything else in their careers.

Talk to any retired mover and shaker and they'll remember the fun they had in business much more vividly than the dramas. Without humour, fun and friendships, a business environment can be boring, to say the least. If you genuinely enjoy people you will find orders easier to achieve, and your business will generally be more efficient.

## CREATING AN ATMOSPHERE

When Hardie took over Reeds in 1978, Keith Davenport, Reeds' Australian chief, suggested I play host to the other divisions so they could present their activities and products to a captive Hardie board. It had all the hallmarks of a tediously long event — so many divisions, so many products, everyone anxious to impress the new owner. It was left to me to lighten it up.

Since the first speakers would be people like the head office financial controller, planning officer and property officer, I guessed the board would be half asleep long before they got to the divisions. So I decided to put a ring-in among the head office speakers, with the fictitious title of Group Purchasing Officer. He was a volunteer from our warehouse, no bigger than a jockey.

He could barely see over the lectern at the presentation.

Shuffling his papers, he read the script we had prepared. "Hello, I'm Fred Jones," he said in a monotone, "... and I do all the purchasing for the Reed Group ... we have 465 cars: 242 Fords, 181 Holdens, 14 Volvos (he proceeded to describe every car down to the last Jaguar) ... we purchase 16 000 tyres per year, 4000 Pirellis, 6000 Bridgestones, 4000 Michelin ..." He then moved on to fuel. The board was stupefied.

Suddenly, the door burst open. Two huge men in white coats swooped in, grabbed an arm each and marched the miserable speaker out, his feet off the ground but still droning on ... and on ... and on ...

After a bemused silence, the board took it in good spirits. It certainly helped make the rest of the presentation a little brighter.

We also had a lot of fun when we launched one of our companies with a Middle-Eastern theme that included camels, Arabian tents and a gorgeous belly dancer. We had a very serious financial director who, caught up in the festive atmosphere, was finally talked into dancing with the belly dancer. We never guessed that when the music started he could make John Travolta seem handicapped.

It brought the house down. The more they clapped and cheered, the more he danced. His spontaneous effort did a lot to show his colleagues that our straight-laced financial man had a human side.

At a dinner party some time later, the financial director and his wife returned to the table after a dance. "You should have seen the display these two put on at the launch of our company the other night," I said to our fellow diners. His wife turned, surprised. Too late I remembered his dancing partner had been the belly dancer!

## EVERYTHING IN MODERATION

Not all attempts to inject fun into business proceedings end so well. I remember a very important occasion, when I was asked to make my yacht available to entertain Sir Alec Jarret, the head of our parent group, Reed International. He was travelling with his personal assistant, Miles, and a few other directors.

We sailed into the Hawkesbury River system and anchored in a beautiful bay. We cooked dinner, drank wine, relaxed and talked.

As we sailed back in the dark, young Miles asked for a spell on the helm. After a while, clearly invigorated by the fresh salt breeze, he asked, "You wouldn't have any rum on board, would you?".

We did, but I warned him that Bundaberg Overproof was a very potent drop before pouring him a glass. Unbeknown to me, he kept asking for more from the cabin, and it wasn't long before I heard the chairman saying, "No, Miles, away from you, Miles. No! No! Towards you Miles!" as his assistant struggled with the tiller. The dreaded Bundy had claimed another victim! My crew carted him below and laid him to rest on one of the bunks.

As we came alongside the wharf at about 1 am, the chairman was still standing behind the tiller. We woke Miles. That was when the rum played its final, cruel trick. Turning an odd shade of green, he rushed too quickly up the companionway into the fresh air, lost control, and sprayed the chairman of the international board with Bundy and a good deal more. Action stations! We raced the chairman ashore and hosed him down on the wharf. A crew member volunteered a clean shirt. Despite our best efforts, however, the smell in the chauffeur-driven car was difficult to ignore.

Poor Miles did not surface for three days. He was still feeling fragile on the last night of his tour when we presented "Kilometre" (not quite a Miles) with six miniature bottles of Bundaberg Rum to mark his visit to Australia. In doing so we managed to lighten up a particularly awkward moment, though I heard soon after that Miles had been rather suddenly transferred to Canada.

## FRIENDS IN BUSINESS

As I move towards the end of my business career, I am grateful for the many friends it has spawned. Many are people who responded to my calls for help without any prospect of immediate gain.

My special friendship with Clyde Packer started in such a manner. When I founded the Hamlyn Group, I was keen to study the reports and balance sheets of every publicly-listed publishing and television company in Australia. I wanted to establish who was who and what was really happening, in order to get a broader view of the market I was entering.

In those days you had to own shares before you could seek

The Macquarie Dictionary *is born. Present (from left) are:*
*university Vice-Chancellor Edwin Webb, John Collins of Jacaranda Press,*
*editor Arthur Delbridge, and the author.*

financial information or reports, so a stockbroker friend began buying one or two shares in hundreds of companies. The trouble started when I became so fed up signing scores of applications that I told him to sign my secretary's name to speed up the process. Though the process was a mere formality, this short cut contravened stock exchange regulations. I learnt my lesson when the secretary of TCN9, who happened to know my secretary, recognised the signature on the share transfer as a forgery and reported it.

My stockbroker mate found himself in real trouble. This was a good, honest man I had put into this predicament. The only man who could save him now, he said, was TCN9 chairman Clyde Packer. This was hardly encouraging, because Clyde was also the chairman of a major competitor, Golden Press. Moreover, there was no love lost between the Packers and Paul Hamlyn, because Paul had cheekily put down Clyde's father on television one night. And in Sydney you don't put down a Packer.

I held my breath and rang Clyde Packer. He said he would see me and I sat, uncomfortably, opposite his big frame.

"What can I do for you?" he said.

"I need your help," I replied.

"Why would I help anyone from the bloody Hamlyn Group?"

"It's not the group, it's me. My best friend is about to be hanged." I explained the situation. "You're the only man who can get him off the hook."

He looked at me searchingly for a while, then went off to his secretary in the next room. I could hear his booming voice. He returned to his seat.

"Your friend is off the hook," he said. "It's fixed."

I was overcome with the compassion of this man, who had been trusting enough to take me at my word. I promised I would never forget his gesture, and I never have. We went on to do some successful joint business projects, share membership in a cellar group and buy a yacht together, though Clyde has never been aboard. He lives for the most part in California these days, but the friendship remains strong. I regard him as a remarkable man — articulate, well read and extremely compassionate. I venture that he is one of the few men who can cross swords with his brother, Kerry.

Charles Scott, former head of the biggest book and magazine distribution company in Australia, Gordon & Gotch, was another valued friend. As number two in the international group, he supported me tremendously when I went out on my own. Not only did Charlie and the boys from Gotch buy my books in the early days, but when I needed it they advanced money before it was due. He was, and is, a special man.

So, too, is Harry Gordon. Years ago I came up with the concept of offering books exclusively through the newspapers of Australia.

Some projects failed, but most were resounding best-sellers — *The Macquarie Dictionary* and *A Day in the Life of Australia* were but two. During this period I met Harry Gordon, who was head of the Brisbane *Courier Mail* at the time. A warm-hearted man, he would always greet you with a bear hug. Harry and I developed a very special friendship and I continue to enjoy his stories and his company. Whenever I have a function that might interest him, he is one of the first on the invitation list.

Recently I had on my property thirty-five international booksellers from countries such as France, Germany, USA, Spain and Sweden. All had to sing their national anthem during the dinner. When the French, to their embarrassment, couldn't get the "Marseillaise" together, Harry did the job for them in fluent French.

Friendship in business? It's the only way to go.

# CHAPTER 20

# Why can't an office be like a home?

*When you move to an empty building, imagine you are going to furnish a series of apartments.*

**K.E.W.**

Why can't an office be like a home? If this sounds like a song, then it should be sung by every office worker in the world. Workers are fed up with air-conditioned cubbyholes in crowded skyscrapers. Enlightened companies are moving into the suburbs and rural belts around the big cities.

## The new moves

I recently studied two large international companies that built low-rise offices and factories north of a big city in order to offer staff a new lifestyle. Before asking them to move, the companies showed them the homes and the lifestyle. They wanted their employees to fall in love with the future before they made the move from a densely populated city to a rural environment where they could acquire bigger homes with swimming pools or waterfront aspects on the same incomes. With the city only an hour away it offered the best of both worlds. It wasn't hard to convince the majority.

Their office changed from a high-rise in a dusty, smoky, industrial suburb to a low-rise bush setting, with rolling lawns and natural bushland teeming with birdlife. With daylight saving, the staff are now able to go sailing, fishing and swimming a hundred metres from their home or office.

Their homes have in many ways become extensions of the office, and the office an extension of their home. They willingly put in extra hours when needed. The productivity of the two companies, huge exporters, has increased enormously.

## How do we make an office a home?

I have never understood who actually approves the building and decorating of some of the new office buildings I see around the world. They may be an architect's dream, but some must be a nightmare to work in. They range from the unfriendly to the sterile and monumental. Furniture tends to be the common office variety because some fool says an office can only function properly if it *looks* like an office.

Try the opposite. When you move to an empty building, imagine you are going to furnish it as a series of apartments. If nothing else, you will go to a home furniture shop instead of an office furniture supplier. You can create cosy corners and a generally calming, colourful *and* functional office. I've moved many times over many years, and it is amazing how our furniture can be shifted around and re-integrated without any great problem, whereas the standard office equipment rarely blends in with a new environment.

## The Hamlyn Group's home

In 1968 I had the power to design an office/warehouse complex. I was determined that it had to have one major ingredient — homeliness. I had purchased an old orchard nursery of 2.5 hectares at Dee Why West. To the left of the property were typical small industrial buildings like fibreglass workshops and small engineering shops. But private homes stood to the right and to the rear, on the slopes that rise to Collaroy Plateau. I felt a responsibility to build a complex that looked more like a large home than a factory. I insisted that a natural spring in the front of the property and the natural bushland down one side be incorporated into the building plan. We spent a lot of money on landscaping and built around the existing trees. At the side of the building we built a large swimming pool and indoor and outdoor eating areas for the staff. Employees could bring their families at

*The author's present office.*

weekends. And they frequently did. In its day, the place looked like a big home.

Over the past ten years my philosophy has been to break the group into the smallest possible units. In Sydney alone we have ten locations. All of them are rather like homes, with the exception of the warehouse complex.

They are, in the main, buildings of historical interest, owned and restored by us. The remainder are terraces or converted homes.

I realise that not all companies can do this. But as we move towards the year 2000, with the inevitable breaking-down of big, bureaucratic companies into smaller units, there will be an exodus from central business districts as organisations seek smaller operating premises. I urge those who make the move to ask themselves, "Why can't an office be like a home?" The answer, as I hope I've displayed, is that it can.

## CHAPTER 21

# NEVER TAKE "NO" FOR AN ANSWER!

*Countless objectives are never reached, simply because those concerned lack the will to persevere.*

**K.E.W.**

You must have the resolve to persevere in business, to hang in to complete the task. When faced with a daunting challenge you will need to rally those around you who either can't be bothered any more, want to forget it because it will *never* work, or believe that even if they finish the job they'll get no more for their efforts. There are even those who view the challenge as the boss's responsibility, not theirs! Yet, with the magic ingredient of perseverance, the "impossible" is achieved remarkably often.

Countless objectives are never reached, simply because those concerned lack the will to persevere. We need only cast our eyes to the arenas of war, business and sport to see the rewards which await those who do.

In the Second World War people achieved tasks considered impossible before the war. They developed radar, set up mass production of bombers and fighters by women, and found a way to weld ships together instead of rivet them. People persevered through bombing raids, day and night, until the tide turned.

In business, perseverance can seem futile in the face of a monopoly, for instance, when it is in fact the only answer. The small, battling company attempting to whittle away at a monopoly needs perseverance more than cash and manpower. I've seen many companies that looked like they would never quite break through.

Yet, with sheer perseverance all their functions eventually clicked into place. Suddenly, after years of heartache, they had made it.

Then there is sport, the arena in which so many business leaders develop their qualities. How often have we seen sporting champions overcome major setbacks, injuries or disabilities that would have crushed lesser hearts? Real champions refuse to acknowledge limits.

I was manager of the Australian Surf Team competing in New Zealand in 1966. The crucial third Test between the two countries was held on the South Island. We had left our competition surfboards on the North Island because we were assured suitable boards would be available. Alas, when the board race came, no board was available for Australia's Barry Rogers. We all gave up hope, except Barry. He grabbed a surf ski, which is much bigger, heavier and slower than a board because it is normally propelled by paddles.

"It can't be done, Barry!" we chorused, not unreasonably.

"I'll give it a go, anyway!" he said stubbornly, and paddled that big, heavy ski around that exhausting course to win the race. As Edgar A. Guest once wrote, "It couldn't be done, but he did it!".

### It Couldn't Be Done

Somebody said that it couldn't be done,
But he with a chuckle replied,
That "maybe it couldn't," but he would be one
Who wouldn't say no till he'd tried.
So he buckled right in with the trace of a grin
On his face. If he worried he hid it.
He started to sing as he tackled the thing
That couldn't be done, and he did it.

Somebody scoffed, "Oh you'll never do that;
At least no one ever has done it";
But he took off his coat and he took off his hat,
And the first thing we knew he'd begun it.
With a lift of his chin and a bit of a grin,
Without any doubt or quiddit,

He started to sing as he tackled the thing
That couldn't be done, and he did it.
There are thousands to tell you it cannot be done,
There are thousands to prophesy failure;
There are thousands to point out to you one by one
The dangers that wait to assail you,
But just buckle in with a bit of a grin
Just take off your coat and go to it;
Just start in to sing as you tackle the thing
That "cannot be done", and you'll do it.

CHAPTER 22

# THE ENVIRONMENTAL SCOURGE

As I grew up, I noticed with dismay how industry had
a total disregard for the environment.

K.E.W.

I was born in a small north Queensland sugar town called Ingham, midway between Townsville and Cairns. My early boyhood was idyllic, particularly the weeks spent camping on nearby Hinchinbrook Island, the largest island national park in the world. There were towering mountains, crystal clear freshwater streams, miles of white sandy beaches and tropical rainforests. I well remember my brothers diving in the creeks for fish that our father had shot with a .303 rifle. We called the place "Our Bush", because in all the years we visited we never saw another person. These years forged my lifetime love of the bush and a clean environment.

As I grew up, I noticed with dismay how industry had a total disregard for the environment and how quickly it became polluted. In the 1950s I saw how factories surrounded by chain-wire fencing housed piles of rusty oil drums and belching smokestacks that would cover your clothes or your mother's washing with soot. Elsewhere, diesel buses coughed out acrid exhaust fumes.

As my understanding of business expanded, I realised that these factories were so appalling because boards and management accepted that dirty factories were the norm. The community simply had to accept pollution as the natural consequence of industry. This attitude prevailed for the next thirty years. During that period I continued to question the ethics of businesses that not only polluted the environment but manufactured products that poisoned, maimed, killed or even threatened humankind.

# Stand up and be counted

Two experiences concerning the role of business in environmental matters left a profound impression on me as a young executive. One was a positive and heroic decision, the other a negative and cowardly one.

Sam Johnson owns the Johnson Wax group of companies, manufacturing in over fifty countries. In the early 1970s, based on evidence that hydrocarbons were destroying the world's ozone layer, he decided to remove sprays using hydrocarbons from all his products.

This brave decision was a world first, costing Johnson Wax millions of dollars. Yet, instead of being applauded by the industry, Sam Johnson was branded irresponsible. When he answered the jibes by delivering a speech entitled "How to Save the World" to the Fortune 500 Club, however, even his detractors had to concede the wisdom of his initiative. Johnson Wax has always been a good corporate citizen — a big company sensitive to the environment and the people.

Not so sensitive was a Canadian paper group which had interests in paper mills worldwide. I was a director of this company's Australian operations when head office decided to build a large newspaper mill in a wilderness area in Canada for about $120 million.

From the outset, the company's treatment of waste entering the rivers was absolutely inadequate. They knew it, but were prepared to pollute rather than spend a few extra million to get it right. Pollution became so serious that the fish on which the local Indians depended for food began to die. Apparently the Indians didn't figure in the company's thinking. As the situation worsened the company's public relations advisers sought to obscure the facts through a campaign of disinformation. They finally came unstuck when the lumberjacks supported the Indians and the plant was closed down for six months while they cleaned up the water. The cost? About 100 times more than it would have been had they fixed it in the first place.

# Government bureaucrats help polluters

How crazy is this world when the anti-pollution arms of some governments allow factories to pollute beautiful surfing beaches by pouring waste into the sea? Such departments actually give permission to companies to dump waste to a certain level. To me, any level is unacceptable. Less surprising is that these companies often exceed the prescribed limit, abetted by dishonest management (not unions!) and irresponsible boards. It seems the biggest offenders are often large, foreign companies, the most tragic example being Union Carbide's poisoning of thousands in Bhopal, India. What good is compensation to the dead? And is the management responsible ever properly punished?

Pat Ken, an ex-British Airways flight attendant, established a home for orphaned children at Dacca in Bangladesh. When asked what she could possibly achieve when the problems were so vast, she quoted, "He who did nothing because it was so little, achieved nothing." Companies and governments do far too little to clean up the environment, using the size of the problem as an excuse.

I discussed the world's shrinking forests one day with US astronaut John Young. He told me that every time he returned from space he saw a clearly-visible reduction of the green on the earth's surface, and fires burning off precious, pristine bush. John Young is in a unique position to know, having been in space more often than any other human being. But are we listening to the space voyager's distressing message? Not very closely, I'm afraid.

But let's be positive. We *have* come a long way in some areas — simple choices like ensuring all company letterhead is printed on recycled paper make a difference. And we will move a lot further if we remain determined to create businesses that are sensitive about the environment and its preservation for future generations.

# CHAPTER 23

# OVERCOMING DISABILITIES

You became more aware of their sheer enthusiasm
than any disability.

**K.E.W.**

When the Second World War ended I bought every book I could about its heroes. Favourites were *Boldness Be My Friend*, *The Dambusters*, and Douglas Bader's autobiography, *Reach For the Sky*. The latter was an enthralling read for a thirteen-year-old. More importantly, it inspired many physically disadvantaged people to face the challenge of their lives.

Douglas Bader, much older than the Battle of Britain pilots he led, lost both his legs in a crash. It should have been the end of any active participation in the war. But not for Bader. In his cocky, self-assured way, he was determined not only to learn to cope, but also to fly again!

After much practice, unfailing courage, and more practice, "Tin Legs" Bader eventually persuaded the brass to let him fly again. Back in Hurricane and Spitfire fighters, he went on to be an ace flyer before being shot down over enemy territory and taken prisoner. Astonishingly he escaped several times, although he was recaptured in each instance. Eventually, despite their admiration for him, the Germans confiscated his legs. It was the only way to stop him.

I spent a week with Sir Douglas Bader and others during an air race in 1971, and cherish the short time I had with him. He was with another great flyer, an American, Frank Tallman, who had a wooden leg. Over a drink in the club bar, Tallman said to Bader, "You know, Douglas, we have only one good leg between us!" (Shortly after that meeting, Tallman was killed landing a plane at his home field in California.)

Both these men, who refused to let their disabilities hinder them in war or peace, distinguished themselves in the business world. And I have known many other business people who have refused to allow any physical disadvantage prevent them becoming very successful in their chosen field.

I once had a young promotions manager working for me who suffered polio in childhood and was left with a noticeably affected right hand. Most people would be inclined to shake hands with their left hand in his situation, but not this fellow. He always extended his right hand, which I'm sure helped him to overcome the disability. He is now managing director and major shareholder of a large film and distribution company.

Another associate had a real problem addressing large groups. His fear was such that he maintained he would resign as chief executive of a large division rather than face an audience. I learned later that he had migrated to Australia from Lebanon as a youngster and every time he had tried to speak in class, other children would heckle him cruelly as a foreigner! Over the years he overcame this problem, to such an extent that he is now an extremely articulate businessman. In fact, a mutual friend said recently that now you can't shut him up!

Imagine a handsome, short, portly man, with thick glasses, a speech impediment and hearing problems. How hard would it be for him to succeed as a book buyer, merchandiser, departmental manager and, finally, the boss of the largest chain of bookshops in Australia? That's what Herb Strathlan did. He had a heart of gold, enormous energy and worked so very, very hard that he overcame his physical disadvantages. His intelligence was certainly no handicap — he could speak and write in eight languages. I loved and admired him, and doing business with him was ever a pleasure.

The quality all these people possessed, in varying degrees, was real grit. You became more aware of their sheer enthusiasm than any disability.

## The inspiration

We all need a strong push now and then to overcome setbacks. Asking "Why me?" never helps. If you can overcome feeling sorry for yourself, it is possible to tackle a wide range of business activities. Technologies such as the fax and the personal computer have opened up new opportunities for disabled people to develop businesses, especially in the service and production industries.

And as an employer, there is absolutely no reason to assume that a physical handicap diminishes the intellect. For proof of this you need look no further than the celebrated but severely handicapped English scientist, Professor Stephen Hawking, who has been compared with Einstein.

## How to employ the handicapped

Examine the functions of your company and ask whether a person in a wheelchair could perform specific tasks — the switchboard, desk work, writing? Then ask whether the company has the facilities to enable them to work. Are there special toilets, ramps, and so on? If not, is the company prepared to install them as the first step towards employing disabled persons? Perhaps this should be mandatory in all sizeable buildings, with a tax rebate incentive for companies prepared to encourage the disabled.

In July 1992, one of the most far-reaching pieces of legislation in years took effect in the USA: the American Disability Act. The Act covers a broad definition of disabilities, from hearing, sight or mobility impairment to emotional illness, dyslexia, AIDS and past drug and alcohol addictions. Under the terms of the Act, it is illegal for businesses to ask job candidates about disabilities. Businesses and governments will have to be miracle workers to adjust the cost of this to industry, but, as with all changes, business will have to face up to it in the future.

Now over ninety years old, American scientist Linus Pauling is the only person ever to win two individual Nobel prizes (chemistry and peace). He said it best:

The reasonable man adapts himself to the World. The unreasonable one persists in trying to adapt the world to himself. Therefore, all progress depends upon the unreasonable man.

# CHAPTER 24

# "GREENFIELDING": STARTING FROM SCRATCH

I met the bank manager with ill-concealed anger.
"Here is my personal situation for the next 12 months.
Do you accept it or not?"

**K.E.W.**

Ideas are easy. Developing the idea into a product or business, creating sales and profit, and then prevailing — that's the difficult part.

"I had that idea!" How often have we heard people say this about a remarkable business success? I've always maintained that any "new" idea for making millions will be shared by countless others all over the world. Only those with the ability to act on those ideas will profit from them.

If you want to start a business, always begin by estimating what it will cost to operate. Start with assumptions if you must, though it is better to accurately detail your operating expenses, beginning with weekly costs. List every cost item if you can. This done, convert the figures to monthly and annual figures. I have found it always pays to overestimate your costs and overestimate the time it takes before sales start coming in. It is a big mistake to be optimistic in this area.

After you have taken this first step you should project for two extra years, using the most detailed figures you can. Then, if it's a manufacturing process, add a detailed product costing.

## FEW PEOPLE FOR STARTERS

Because so much of starting a new business is guesswork, most businesses end up bigger than first envisaged, not smaller. A cardinal mistake is to employ too many people too soon and later find they have to be dismissed. Start with a very small team and add new people very, very selectively. Contract out as much work as possible until you are convinced that it can be more profitably handled in house.

Don't rush to buy capital items too quickly either. Hire or lease in the short term until your capital requirements are properly known.

## QUICK SALES CAN SEND YOU BROKE

The urge we all have to expand quickly has pushed many new companies over the edge. It's called "over-trading". New people in new businesses don't seem to understand that if you get large sales very quickly you need more money from the bank to pay your creditors and give customers that much more credit. In other words, you find yourself with insufficient working capital to service an expanding balance sheet.

## CASH FLOW

The key to a successful new venture is to understand the magic words "cash flow". It should be rubber stamped on every employee's forehead, and flash from rooftop neon signs: cash flow ... cash flow ... cash flow.

Most people who start new companies, other than accountants (and even *they* regularly stuff it up), get confused with cash flow figures. Yet it is really a very simple exercise that must be understood.

When I was first married, money was tight. It was to be the first and last time a bank stopped a cheque of mine. I had so many bills one month that I went into overdraft for the princely sum of $15 and the next cheque was bounced. I was so upset that I documented all my monthly outgoings for a twelve-month period — adding and subtracting my wages — before confronting the bank manager. The twelve-month picture showed I would be slightly overdrawn for only two months.

Once in the bank manager's office I said, with ill-concealed anger, "Here is my personal situation for the next twelve months. Do you accept this or not?" He was very impressed and I never suffered the indignity of a bounced cheque again.

What I had done was create my own very detailed cash flow. Every month I put down my actual outgoings next to my monthly estimates, adjusting if I had to. When we talk about cash flow in business this is basically what it is all about. Every month you record what you spend against what you receive. You either need money from the bank, or elsewhere, or you put money in the bank, or elsewhere.

## Listing all outgoings and all incoming revenues

Incoming Revenue is not the Sales Invoiced but the Cash Received. Cash Out is not the Invoice Received but the Cash Paid Out. Having done this simple exercise, you must allocate time to project three months forward as a re-forecast, to ensure that you won't have a blowout.

## Spend time on projections

It is imperative to spend time projecting correct cash flows so you can anticipate if you will blow out three months down the road. Your bank manager may be more sympathetic if you can show you are in control.

I draft three plans when I start a new business:

*Plan 1* estimates overheads on the high side and projects pessimistic sales.

*Plan 2* is realistic about overheads and sales.

*Plan 3* is low on overheads and optimistic about sales.

I usually fall somewhere between Plan 1 and 2, or Plan 2 and 3, but like to gear up for Plan 1 with the energy and enthusiasm to achieve Plan 2.

## Ask for help

Most people who start new companies seem reluctant to ask customers, staff and suppliers for help and guidance. Some feel it is beneath their dignity. But I have found that people respond positively if you are genuine. For instance, if cash is short a proper, private request to collect a cheque from a customer a little early is often favourably received.

In the early days ask staff to work longer hours until the company gets established. This should be balanced with a genuine promise of sharing the fruit — if there *is* fruit on the sideboard — in the future. Suppliers, if approached with humility, can sometimes help by extending payments or splitting shipments.

When I was given the role of establishing the Paul Hamlyn group in Australia in 1967, I contacted Bill Simmons, a man for whom I had great admiration. He was then chairman and chief executive officer of Straits Times Press, a very large and successful newspaper and magazine publishing group in Singapore. I had done a little business with him in my previous job and when I asked for extended terms for the printing of *Australia's Heritage* he responded magnificently. From that moment he adopted me like a son, giving me enormous help and advice until the day he retired.

## THE BIG TRAP IN GREENFIELDING

Remember the Simon Gompertz quote: "There is only one thing worse than losing money, that's thinking you are making money when you are losing it." This usually occurs when proper provisions and write-offs are not made, when products are sold at discounted margins without the adjustments being made to gross profit, or when costs are overlooked. Deferred payables are another trap for the unwary, because by the time they are recognised the company may have already embarked on developing product that is bound to be unprofitable.

## THE RIGHT MARGIN

Many businesses start with overheads so high and margins so low that even outstanding sales will provide insufficient return on their investments.

The converse is also a common mistake with new businesses. They charge too much for their product. Remember, the world is full of multi-millionaires who sold their product too cheaply! So don't be greedy when you start selling a product or service. Later, if the service and quality are still there, you can slowly increase your price. It is very difficult to lower your price later if you have charged too much from the start.

## Quality

Whatever your product or service, you must aim for quality of service and product at an affordable price to give yourself a fair chance.

## The Right People

It is understood that the right people are essential but it takes time to build a good team. If some don't work out, it is essential to have the strength — and the compassion — to let these people go before they put the business at risk.

## Success in Marketing

This is simply the right product, the right price, the right place at the right time with the right promotion (see also Chapter 7).

## The Right Product

It should be accepted that your service or product is right and that there is a need for it. If there isn't you are doomed. It will be difficult enough in any event, even if you are offering something that is unique, of sound quality and of perceived value. If your product is innovative, then it will not be as price sensitive.

## The Right Price

This is obviously what the market can stand. Bear in mind that if your product is the same as others, but cheaper, your opposition will eventually come down in price to meet yours. Price alone may not be enough to ensure your product's success.

## The Right Place

Too many companies put their product or service into a market that isn't right for the consumer. Perhaps the product is not placed where they can see it. This is where the method of distribution of your product is crucial — direct to user, retail or wholesale? This must be decided before you start your business, because of the different margins involved. If the product is being heavily promoted through the media, the product must flood the marketplace so the consumer can respond. Too often product well promoted on television cannot be found in the stores.

## THE RIGHT TIME

Timing is essential for success in business. Putting a new product on the market too soon or too late is disastrous. "They were ahead of their time — look how successful it is now!" How often have we heard this after the original company went broke.

An example that springs to mind is a record company we once launched that did very well. Soon after, the eight-track cassette and the Philips standard audio cassette were launched to compete with the LP record. Had we rushed to convert all our LPs to cassettes, we would have been too early. We slowed up new additions to our list until cassette-players were sold in sufficient numbers to create demand for the new cassettes.

Being too late, of course, is just as bad. We have all seen the demise of department stores that refused to join the move to large regional shopping centres, preferring to remain in central business districts.

## THE RIGHT PROMOTION

This is a difficult subject because different promotional techniques are needed for each product. But the options fall into pretty simple categories. First consider the following:

- Does the product look a quality product?
- Does the product have a good name?
- Does the product have a good price?
- Does the product transport easily?
- Does the product rack and display readily?

If all of the above look reasonable, you should move to the next stage, which is to design an attractive package and then decide what promotion you will pursue. This may be by way of:

- Direct mail leaflets
- Direct mail TV

- TV promotion
- Newspapers and magazines
- Trade journals or magazines
- Household drops
- Radio
- Billboards
- Theatre

The best promotion is the personal recommendation. Just look at Christianity. Once founded, it took only ten years for the then known world to learn about it. People kept telling their friends, and they in turn told their friends about this wonderful new product. Some promotion!

## Advantages of starting up . . .

There are clear advantages in starting a new business, compared to taking over an existing one. You rarely have to outlay large sums to acquire a new business, you don't inherit bad company policies, antiquated product or established systems, and you don't have to cope with resentful staff if you try to alter entrenched practices.

In general, I have found it more financially rewarding to start a new company than acquire one.

## . . . and the disadvantages

It usually takes several years before a new company is properly established, with good production, good people and good systems.

When I started the Hamlyn Group, my late father, who had been in business, said it would take five years before I got it right. Silly old bugger, I thought. I'm only thirty and I'll move much more quickly. I did for a while, then fell back, then went forward. It *was* five years before I felt I had the right people, systems and product.

Business advisers worry about companies that grow rapidly. So they should. But I have found that, providing you judge it right, you should just pull back on large growth rates for a year. Set lower sales targets, pull back the overheads to match the ratio to reduced sales and "clean up the house".

Do a thorough management audit. Revalue assets down, write-off, sell off, tighten up. When I did this, the staff felt relieved of the burden of chasing impossibly high targets. The easier targets made them feel more confident and, to everyone's amazement, we sustained the same high growth rate! But we achieved it in a more considered and relaxed manner. This action firms up the future for a business.

## SUCCESS OVER THE LONG TERM

Low borrowings, strong positive cash flows and balance sheet values that reflect a realistic value — these are the components that put a business on track for the longer haul.

In my early years, I was appalled by the number of people I knew who failed in new businesses.

"How is business going?"

"Great, I made $100 000 profit."

Six months later they were in trouble. Why didn't their accountant, when determining their profit, indicate that unless they provided for $50 000 tax and a $100 000 annual interest bill they'd be broke in six months? What good is paper profit without a positive cash flow to pay the bills?

## STARTING A BUSINESS FOR CAPITAL GAIN

I know a few people who have made little money from new businesses, but have sold their company for huge sums. A friend in the US has owned or held shares in various baseball teams. The investment offers no cash flow, but he always makes lots of money on the sale.

Some invest with the express purpose of selling. Big corporations, for instance, sometimes buy new companies solely to remove them from competition.

There is a funny story about Abe, who saw his neighbour, Ben, backing a big, loaded truck into his yard.

"Ben!" said Abe, "What ya got in the truck?"

"Sardines," said Ben, "Just bought them for a bargain — 20 cents a tin!"

"Wanna sell them, Ben?" said Abe.

"Yep — 25 cents a tin"

"Done," said Abe, and took delivery. Abe was then backing the truck into his shed when his cousin Eddie called in.

"Abe!" said Eddie, "What ya got in the truck?"

"Sardines," said Abe, "I just bought them for a bargain — 25 cents a tin!"

"Wanna sell them Abe?" said Eddie.

"Yep — 30 cents a tin."

"Done," said Eddie, and took them away.

Two days later Eddie returned to Abe. He was very annoyed. "Abe," he said, "I opened one of the tins and the sardines were rotten, useless! I want my money back!"

"Eddie," said Abe patiently, "Those sardines were for buying and selling, not for eating!"

I know a few companies that over the past twenty years have never been very successful, but they somehow keep being bought and sold.

## The Right Attitude

The most important qualities you need when starting a new business are faith in yourself, determination, patience and perseverance. Remember the adage, "Success without hard work or profit without risk has not yet been invented." If you are not prepared to work hard or take risks, don't bother.

The following has been extracted in part from a recent article in the USA, "How to Grow and Survive from Scratch by Substituting Imagination and Know-How in an Effort for Capital".

- *New niche*: Get into a new business at the dawn of an era. New niches pop up with regularity these days.
- *Tap vendors*: When business is tough, vendors and suppliers can be convinced to give credit in kind, such as free rent for a year, or to supply information that might enable you to get a particular job.
- *Do consulting*: Countless businesses have been launched on initial revenues radiating from consulting contracts. (It was how I started my own business. My consultancy fees paid my total

operating overheads so that, with any book I published, my gross profit became my net profit. Great if you can get it.)

- *Vacant areas*: Establish in areas with lots of vacancies and empty buildings. You'll always get a good deal.
- *Advertise*: Take an ad out and see what happens. Providing you don't lash out on prime-time TV, a small ad in the right place at start up can produce amazing results.
- *Employ craftsmen who have their own tools and equipment*: This keeps the capital outlay down and overheads low.
- *Get customers to pay fast*: Many companies are sympathetic to paying faster if you are a small operation that has just started.
- *Coddle suppliers*: Get your own suppliers to help with staggered deliveries using their infrastructure (warehousing, production lines, finance).
- *Sell wholesale*: Sell wholesale and source a bigger area than if you are trying to sell retail. This will reduce margins, but it can give you quick volume and many retail outlets, and this helps keep overheads down.
- *Do it yourself*: Don't be quick to hire managers to run your business. Do it yourself.
- *Try to look bigger than you are*: Sometimes new businesses struggle because of the perception that they are small and may disappear. There is nothing wrong with making your business look bigger. [When I started, I called my company Kevin Weldon & Associates. The name implied there were lots of us — in reality, it was just me and my secretary. I took a bigger office and sub-let sections so that there were always a lot of people about. You only need to do this until you make it.]
- *Ask several banks at the same time for a loan*: This must be done simultaneously, as one refusal will go against the other.
- *A little begging goes a long way*: Don't be too proud to ask your clients for a little up-front money. Certainly pick up the phone if they are late for payment. (When I went out on my own, I was never too shy to ask for a little bit after fifteen days. I received great support, some clients paying 25 per cent on delivery.)
- *Perform cheap market research*: Take your invention, product or

service, and test it on your relations, friends, neighbours and people in the street. You'll get good feedback and it won't cost you much. More importantly, you'll learn first hand, not through some academic research organisation.

- *Multi-supplier channels*: It is sometimes impossible to obtain large credit from one supplier, so you should consider small amounts from many suppliers. It spreads the risk of one supplier being concerned about you.
- *Change of direction*: Sometimes a business doesn't succeed, but a function or a part-product will take off. An example is the lady who started Z-Barten productions. Her greeting cards were costly to produce and she decided to stick collages all over them and sprinkle them with glitter. Her customers kept asking her where she got the sparkles. Barten saw the light. She became a full-time sparkle-maker.

The story of Johnson Wax is a much larger example. When it was founded, it made and installed parquetry flooring and produced a wax to polish them. Everyone kept asking for Johnson's wax, to the point where the company abandoned floors in the 1920s to concentrate on waxes and sprays.

Avon was started as a door-to-door book-selling business which gave away cosmetics with the books. Soon the demand for its cosmetics was such that it abandoned books to become one of the largest cosmetics companies in the world.

- *Say, "Can do"*: Too often deals are lost when the client asks for a delivery by a certain date and the quick answer is "no". Deal lost. Try "Yes, I can deliver a sizeable quantity and the balance over such-and-such a period." Be quick to find a way to say, "Can do", not "Can't do". It's amazing what can be done.

## SOME CAUTIONARY THOUGHTS

You may feel under pressure to cut corners when your company's survival is at stake. The first thing that can go is your ethics and integrity — and your integrity is challenged daily by the promises you make. Do you make promises you know you can't keep? Here's a quote from *Business Magazine*:

> What we learned, and what all too many new businessmen can miss, is that being truthful is good business. You may solve some temporary bind by fibbing, but it will come back to haunt you. It's not just wrong — it also doesn't work.

While Marshall & Thicker said in *Thinking for a Living*:

> Competition is a high-tech global economy. It stresses quality, service and speed. This cannot be achieved by grinding out the most product at the lowest cost. Workers at the point of production from the factory hand to the sales clerk must think and act for themselves.

Most British and Australian managers are mired in the mind-set of mass production, enthusiastically slashing costs instead of boosting quality and production. Keep this in mind when starting a new business.

# CHAPTER 25

# MANAGEMENT: FROM EVOLUTION TO REVOLUTION

... where people can touch each other, care about each other
more, and, much more importantly, make
decisions in their own right.

K.E.W.

The demand for goods and services after the Second World War was so great that it exceeded the world's capacity to supply them. The USA, now the most powerful nation, responded by pouring its energies into mass production. Japan and Germany soon followed suit under America's stewardship. Thus business organisation became pyramid-shaped, with management in complete charge — Toffler's "smokestack mentality". The days of the manager who handled everything from accounts to sales had passed.

When I entered the junior management area in the early 1950s Drucker's "Scientific Management" held sway. Everything and everybody was pigeon-holed. In Australia, management courses were introduced to technical colleges for the first time. It was management by textbook.

Those same textbooks quoted consultants at London's Tavistock Institute, who advised business leaders to give their workers, particularly technicians, more responsibility in factories. Factory and office guidebooks followed, with Drucker's *Scientific Manager Advisory* and *Motion and Time Study Work Committee* both setting out work practices emphasising the role of the worker. Nevertheless, the response of business to this empowerment of the worker was very slow through the 1950s and 1960s.

Then, in the 1970s, the potential of the individual was suddenly acknowledged, with less reliance on established systems and a new emphasis on personal development.

Unfortunately, while the workers were finally being recognised as an asset, managerial specialists had already burrowed deep into the tissue of business.

The 1960s had seen the rise of the specialist in industry, and by the early 1970s financial and technical engineering specialists were crowding into management roles. The chief executive officer was now surrounded by specialists — the chief financial officer, the personnel officer, the technical officer, the communications officer and the advertising expert. The so-called leader relinquished a goodly portion of the decision-making by delegating to specialists. Businesses all over the world were drowning in specialists.

Bureaucracy in business had begun in earnest. Instead of improving decision-making at any level, it expanded middle management to further swell the bureaucratic structure, taking decision-making further and further from its proper place — out there in the front line.

The philosophies underpinning mass production might have served us well when a large proportion of auto workers and the like were uneducated immigrants. But as the education of the workforce improved, its members became demoralised by the same mindless tasks, without any understanding or appreciation of their role in the total operation. The system no longer worked.

Management training, one of the growth businesses in the 1970s, clearly failed here. The management techniques it promoted simply did not work, because the old organisation chart remained largely unchanged, except for specialist circles being added to each of the old squares. The result? More people shuffling more paper so the boss could make the final decision. Decision-making slowed as a stumbling and inefficient middle management, replete with specialists, grew and grew.

Workers who had been given hope of a new order in the early 1970s soon found themselves stifled by this burgeoning bureaucracy. They had every right to feel cheated.

# THE JAPANESE WAY

In the late 1970s the astonishing success of Japanese industry inspired many Western companies to advocate the Japanese management system as the new way. It was, I believe, a mistake. Few appreciated that Japanese industry was set on course by the American management consultant W. Edward Deaming, who, with others, decided to help the Japanese when their own countrymen spurned their ideas. Deaming and his colleagues encountered a unique environment, one in which military defeat had galvanised the nation's determination to prevail.

The climate was very different thirty years on. The inherent inefficiency of bureaucracies, coupled with the need for greater corporate flexibility and Japan's persistent overcrowding problem, saw Japanese companies beginning to dismantle the very monolithic organisations we were belatedly trying to emulate.

Today, Japanese business, as part of the national objective, sees a need to establish as many companies, offices and branches outside Japan as possible. This ensures that as many staff as practicable reside overseas, living off the host country's infrastructure and creating, where possible, support and service companies for their own use. These companies also establish their own transport companies, food (particularly meat-producing) companies and, of late, their own tour guides in foreign countries for their own nationals. Japanese deals in foreign lands are very often deals that will get more of their people out of their own crowded land.

On the home front, Japan has already begun to break down many of its big bureaucratic companies. Fujitsu, the second largest computer company after IBM, is floundering, profits diminishing in the face of competition from smaller personal computer producers. Asahi Nippon, one of the largest insurance companies in the world, is already breaking itself down into smaller units.

Believe me, Japan is under just as much pressure to collapse its bureaucracy as the rest of the world. Their management style, so suitable and successful in the past, is too inflexible for the future.

# Industrial Relations

During the early 1980s businesses around the world, particularly in Australia, suffered severe industrial unrest. Very high levels of employment had created a labour shortage, which in turn resulted in management and workers bargaining for ridiculous rewards. In my opinion, this was not so much a product of proletarian greed — as some would have it — as a consequence of management's continuing unwillingness to deal intelligently with their employees' elected representatives, the unions.

I had my own experience of this almost ten years earlier. In 1975 the head of Reed, Sir Don Ryder, sent me to the UK (with other young managers from the old colonies of Canada and South Africa) to be let loose on various Reed companies suffering industrial strife and poor productivity. The main problem was immediately apparent — too many management specialists, personnel managers, and what I called the middle management (or "middle counties snobs" when I felt less charitable).

The fundamental bone of contention was that employees needed to work twenty hours overtime a week to receive the miserly income of £43 needed to pay for housing commission rent, a pint of bitter and food. To ensure they all worked the extra twenty hours employees (not surprisingly) conspired to work slowly during the standard forty hours. Reed was working one-and-a-half shifts a day on a base rate of £32 a week at this plant. The German opposition, which paid a base rate of £43 and ran three shifts twenty-four hours a day, was killing us.

When I saw the blackboard presentation from the personnel department on how we paid our workers, it showed £32 plus a lot of complicated computations. "What did the workers' representative say when you detailed this formula for him?" I asked.

"He said he didn't understand it, sir," the buffoon replied. Why would he understand it? I certainly didn't. What we had was a group of "experts" trying to confuse the workers with their cleverness in order to deny them a better deal.

Management "experts" were also at the root of a hurtful strike in the early 1980s. Our major distributor had an industrial stoppage at its main warehouse in Melbourne. It cost publishers a disastrous portion of the Christmas trade. Management blamed it on "the bloody Storemen and Packers' Union", but I was determined to find out why this Melbourne company had been singled out. Had the management negotiated? No! Was the branch manager the type to talk to the workers at their own level? No! He was the conservative financial type, not one to sort things out at the pub with the workers.

The final miscalculation was that talks with the workers were conducted by an industrial relations consultant who came from an area with the worst industrial relations record in Australia. Not a good start. Of course it ended badly.

## New beginning

Ten years ago my own grass roots experience and study of management led me to create a business structure that has served Weldon International extremely well. We still have a long way to go in the human relations department — more managers need to be able to lead and motivate rather than rule by power alone — but we *are* organised into small, flexible, decision-making units. It was a thrill to read Toffler's recent book, *Power Shift*, and find his articulation of a business philosophy we embraced many years earlier.

As Toffler says, we are in a business environment at the threshold of a major revolution that will see:

- The breakdown of huge bureaucracies; decision-making devolving to the lowest possible level in small units; and increasing use of the present technology if we are to succeed.
- The collapse of what Toffler calls the "smokestack" mentality.

Middle management must be reduced, and the best of them made managers of small flexible units where people can touch each other, care about each other and, much more importantly, make decisions in their own right. This revolution has begun. Companies that don't make these changes are unlikely be around in the future.

# CHAPTER 26

# SLASHING THE RED TAPE

It ain't easy to break down bureaucracy. But the hardest part
is finding the courage to tackle it.

**K.E.W.**

Let me say here and now, it *ain't* easy to break down bureaucracy.
But the hardest part is finding the courage to tackle it.

How does a company become a bureaucracy in the first place? It
starts with head office centralising all financial services, planning,
strategies, personnel departments, group purchasing, travel,
computers and so on. Head office then charges or spreads those
costs throughout its operational units.

The operational units complain continually about these
charges, but keep using the central services instead of arranging
their own travel, building maintenance, or personal computers. A
bureaucracy is born.

I once tried to dismantle the head office of a company I had
taken over. Some positions simply disappeared because there was
no longer any need for them. But it was only after shifting all the
companies involved out of a big, central office/warehouse
complex that I started to make real progress. Try as I might, I
could not complete the breakdown until each separate business
had its own premises. Those in the unnecessary bureaucracy
found themselves isolated with no central activity. Total collapse
was completed.

Don't automatically assume there is no future for the people
made redundant, however. They should be employed in different
roles in the units. For example, a central computer person may be a
productive manager in a unit. And so on.

# NEED FOR GROUP ACTIVITIES

Sometimes it's impractical to close down a group function immediately. I have had some success transferring a group function to a separate unit, which then charges the service *back* to head office. A head office task such as a central consolidation of the group's monthly figures, for instance, might be performed by the figure person in that small unit as an extra duty. Charging their time back to head office in this first stage is cheaper than supplying offices and assistance at head office. Eventually such tasks may be absorbed by the unit as a normal function.

Appointing units to take over central functions removes the blight of specialists in head office. These specialists might appear when a group has to examine a new business or process, head office immediately creating a whole new empire to handle it. The new department may be called "research and development" or "special projects".

This is the wrong way to go. It just builds an empire full of people either not commercial enough or too far removed from the front line. Give the task to a selected unit instead. Not only will they learn from the experience, but they have the benefit of being closer to the market. Too often, top management seems to believe that they need a lot of people on their floor in order to function properly. Some feel the need to have people running into their offices, advising and seeking advice, in the hope of becoming better managers and decision-makers. It is a forlorn hope.

Ronald Reagan built up quite a reputation as the Governor of California by vetoing plans to build a massive building to house the bureaucracy. He slashed the workforce instead, and was thereby able to use less of the building they already occupied. He made some departments smaller, abolished others, reduced the budget expenditure and increased efficiency. He could never have achieved this if he had built that huge new bureaucratic edifice.

# CHAPTER 27

# STATING THE MISSION

A company must understand its reason for being.

**K.E.W.**

Management by Vision is a management concept in which the broader aspirations of a company are clearly articulated for all employees. I call it a Vision Statement. Most companies call it "The Mission Statement".

A mission statement is prepared for the owners by the chief executive officer. The CEO must sincerely believe the contents and, if necessary, be prepared to change their ways to conform with the statement. Employees are frequently consulted before determining the final contents.

A typical start to framing a mission statement is to ask some of the questions posed by Bob Wall, Robert S. Solum and Mark R. Sobol in their book, *The Visionary Leader*:

- Why does the company exist anyway?
- How do we work together?
- Who do we work for?
- What do we do?
- Who are we?
- Where do we fit in the community?
- What, as a group, do we really care about?
- What don't we like about other businesses?
- What don't we like about other business leaders?
- What do we like about other business leaders?
- Would your mother be proud of what you do and how you do it?

Add other questions that may be appropriate to your business.

## THE FUNCTIONS

The functions of a mission statement are manifold. In order to realise its full potential, a company must first understand its reason for being. Secondly, it must have a sense of direction. Rodale Press, for instance, aims "to publish books that empower people's lives". This leaves everyone in the company in no doubt about their goal.

The mission statement must engender sufficient enthusiasm for the staff to embrace the company's goal as their own goal. If the vision is crystal clear, all else will fall into place. Without a stated vision, a company's sense of direction can become blurred or confused.

An inspired mission statement should also stimulate productivity and creativity. Another function is to clarify procedures for employees.

Take Sears Department Store in the US as an example. Their large vehicle repair section was ordered by the Federal Court to pay $8 million to customers it had dishonestly overcharged for car repairs. How could this possibly have happened? Someone with authority must have misled their colleagues into believing it would be okay if they could get away with it. In this case, a mission statement from the highest authority would have left no-one in doubt about the company's ethics and could have prevented such a travesty.

## GETTING THE MESSAGE ACROSS

Once you have completed your mission statement, you face three hurdles:

- Getting your people to live and abide by it.
- Convincing *all* your people why you need it.
- Making them understand it.

Start by outlining the vision to each manager, preferably in informal surroundings away from the office. Some will absorb it without difficulty. Others will have to be persuaded to adjust their thinking and their ways. Some will be unable to believe in the mission, or adjust to new ways. If they are considered hard-working and important employees, try to find them a new position where they might adjust. If they are neither, they must go. If you are ambivalent about this your people will doubt either your commitment or the substance of the mission statement — or both!

Some suggest that everyone should memorise the mission statement. I don't go along with this, but if it is kept simple and genuine they will remember it anyway.

Next, get these managers to work with their teams. They should explain the statement, encourage discussion and ask where, in the team's opinion, the company fails to meet the goals of the statement. This whole process should be carried out thoroughly so that everyone is convinced to make a commitment to the mission statement.

It is imperative that all managers embrace the mission statement before seeking the commitment of all employees. If you need to change your company, fire people, or accept a short-term loss of profits to get the mission statement universally accepted, then you must — otherwise you will fail in the long run.

In my opinion, the following mission statements, including that of Weldon International, offer good examples of their kind. Rodale Press is a family-owned book and magazine publishing company in Pennsylvania, while the Johnson Wax group of companies manufactures in more than fifty countries.

## THE RODALE PRESS BOOKS MISSION STATEMENT

*Our mission*
We publish books that empower people's lives.

*Our principles and objectives*
### Customer satisfaction
We will establish long-term customer relationships by offering products that inspire and instruct — products that are editorially unique, factually accurate, and graphically appealing.

We are committed to developing and maintaining high-quality customer service as a long-term strategy to retain customers.

We are committed to improving our understanding of our customers — what they buy from us, why they buy it, and how we can meet their needs.

We will develop quantifiable methods to target customers with the products they want most, thereby increasing their long-term satisfaction.

We will continue to build a positive image within the community, within our industry, and with our customers.

We are committed to the highest standard of ethical conduct in all our relationships.

## Product quality

We will continually challenge ourselves to create more value in every product — value that meets or exceeds the expectations of our targeted market.

We recognise that downgrading the quality of our editorial product to meet profit margins may have a long-term effect on our customer and employee satisfaction; therefore, we will develop effective procedures to review all cost-driven decisions.

We recognise that value is created by a combination of editorial quality, product price and customer service. We will continually strive to improve our understanding and management of these components so that our customers perceive our products to be valuable and competitive in the current marketplace.

## Employee development

Our most important asset is the talent and satisfaction of our employees. We are committed to attracting, developing, and retaining quality employees by:

- Fostering an open, supportive, and creative management environment;
- Developing educational and training opportunities;
- Providing timely financial and career rewards for quality performance; and
- Delegating authority and responsibility.

We recognise the importance of our unique corporate culture and are committed to its constant nurturance and reinforcement.

We are committed to equal employment opportunity.

## Financial management

We are committed to increasing the profitability of our core business. We will place a high priority on growing our earnings through product development and acquisition.

We will continue to develop, utilise and expand our information-based marketing capabilities in order to facilitate growth.

We recognise the importance of developing integrated marketing and financial reporting systems to effectively control all business functions.

We recognise the importance of long-term strategic planning and are committed to it.

We recognise that clear organisational and reporting structures facilitate the achievement of our goals.

## THE JOHNSON WAX MISSION STATEMENT

*This We Believe*

> "The goodwill of the people is the only enduring thing in any business. It is the sole substance ... The rest is shadow!"

> *H. F. Johnson, Sr*

*Introduction*

Our company has been guided by certain basic principles since its founding in 1886. These principles were first summarised in 1927 by H.F. Johnson, Sr, in his Christmas Profit Sharing speech:

> "The goodwill of the people is the only enduring thing in any business. It is the sole substance . . . The rest is shadow!"

In 1976, we formally stated these basic principles in "This We Believe". Since then, our statement of corporate philosophy has been translated and communicated around the world — not only within the worldwide company, but also to key external audiences. It has served us well by providing all employees with a common statement of the basic principles which guide the company in all the different cultures where we operate. It has also provided people outside the company with an understanding of our fundamental beliefs. It communicates the kind of company we are.

Now, more than ten years after "This We Believe" was developed, and following the celebration of our 100th anniversary, it is appropriate to restate, clarify and reaffirm our commitment to uphold these principles, because our company, like most others in these highly volatile times, has had to adjust its business strategies worldwide. This restatement and clarification is important to ensure that our corporate policies and the actions of our managers and other employees continue to be fully supportive of our beliefs.

"This We Believe" states our benefits in relation to the five groups of people to whom we are responsible and whose trust we have to earn:

*Employees*
We believe that the fundamental vitality and strength of our worldwide company lies in our people.

*Consumers and users*
We believe in earning the enduring goodwill of consumers and users of our products and services.

*General public*
We believe in being a responsible leader within the free market economy.

*Neighbours and hosts*
We believe in contributing to the well-being of the countries and communities where we conduct business.

*World community*
We believe in improving international understanding.
These beliefs are real and we will strive to live up to them. Our commitment to them is evident in our actions to date.

The sincerity of our beliefs encourages us to act with integrity at all times, to respect the dignity of each person as an individual human being, to assume moral and social responsibilities early as a matter of conscience, to make an extra effort to use our skills and resources where they are most needed, and to strive for excellence in everything we do.

Our way of safeguarding these beliefs is to remain a privately held company. Our way of reinforcing them is to make profits through growth and development, profits which allow us to do more for all the people on whom we depend.

We believe that the fundamental vitality and strength of our worldwide company lies in our people, and we commit ourselves to:

- Maintain good relations among all employees around the world based on a sense of participation, mutual respect, and an understanding of common objectives, by:
  - Creating a climate whereby all employees freely air their concerns and express their opinions with the assurance that these will be fairly considered.
  - Attentively responding to employees' suggestions and problems.
  - Fostering open, two-way communications between management and employees.
  - Providing employees with opportunities to participate in the process of decision-making.
  - Encouraging employees at all levels and in all disciplines to work as a team.
  - Respecting the dignity and rights of privacy of every employee.

- Manage our business in such a way that we can provide security for regular employees and retirees, by:
  - Pursuing a long-term policy of planned, orderly growth.
  - Retaining regular employees, if at all possible, as conditions change. However, this may not always be possible, particularly where major restructuring or reorganisation is required to maintain competitiveness.
  - Retraining employees who have acceptable performance records and are in positions no longer needed, provided suitable jobs are available.

- Maintain a high level of effectiveness within the organisation, by:
  - Establishing clear standards of job performance.
  - Ensuring that the performance of all employees meets required levels by giving appropriate recognition to those

whose performance is good and by terminating those whose performance, despite their managers' efforts to help, continues below company standards.

- Provide equal opportunities in employment and advancement, by:
  - Hiring and promoting employees without discrimination, using qualifications, performance and experience as the principle criteria.
- Remunerate employees at levels that fully reward their performance and recognise their contribution to the success of their company, by:
  - Maintaining base pay and benefit programs, both of which are fully competitive with those prevailing within the relevant marketplaces.
  - Maintaining, in addition to our fully competitive pay and benefit programs, our long-standing tradition of sharing profits with employees.
- Protect the health and safety of all employees, by:
  - Providing a clean and safe work environment.
  - Providing appropriate safety training and occupational health services.
- Develop the skills and abilities of our people, by:
  - Providing on-the-job training and professional development programs.
  - Helping employees qualify for opportunities in the company through educational and development programs.
- Create environments which are conducive to self-expression and personal well-being, by:
  - Fostering and supporting leisure-time programs for employees and retirees.
  - Developing job-enrichment programs.
  - Maintaining the long tradition of high quality and good design in our offices and plants.
- Encourage initiative, innovation, and entrepreneurism among all employees, thereby providing opportunities for greater job

satisfaction while also helping the worldwide company achieve its objectives.

We believe in earning the enduring good will of consumers and users of our products and services, and we commit ourselves to:

- Provide useful products and services throughout the world, by:
  - Monitoring closely the changing wants and needs of consumers and users.
  - Developing and maintaining high standards of quality.
  - Developing new products and services which are recognised by consumers and users as being significantly superior overall to major competition.
  - Maintaining close and effective business relations with the trade to ensure that our products and services are readily available to consumers and users.
  - Continuing our research and development commitment to provide a strong technology base for innovative and superior products and services.

- Develop and market products which are environmentally sound and which do not endanger the health and safety of consumers and users, by:
  - Meeting all regulatory requirements or exceeding them where worldwide company standards are higher.
  - Providing clear and adequate directions for safe use, together with cautionary statements and/or symbols.
  - Incorporating protection against misuse where this is appropriate.
  - Researching new technologies for products which favour an improved environment.

- Maintain and develop comprehensive education and service programs for consumers and users, by:
  - Disseminating information to consumers and users which promotes full understanding of the correct use of our products and services.
  - Handling all inquiries, complaints, and service needs for consumers and users quickly, thoroughly and fairly.

- We believe in being a responsible leader in the free market economy, and we commit ourselves to:
- Ensure the future vitality of the worldwide company, by:
  - Earning sufficient profits to provide new investment for planned growth and progress.
  - Maintaining a worldwide organisation of highly competent, motivated and dedicated employees.
- Conduct our business in a fair and ethical manner, by:
  - Not engaging in unfair business practices.
  - Treating our suppliers and customers both fairly and reasonably, according to sound commercial practice.
  - Packaging and labelling our products so that consumers and users can make informed, valued judgements.
  - Maintaining the highest advertising standards of integrity and good taste.
  - Not engaging in bribery.
- Share the profits of each local company with those who have contributed to its success, by:
  - Rewarding employees through a profit-sharing program.
  - Allocating a share of the profits to enhance the well-being of communities where we operate.
  - Developing better products and services for the benefit of consumers and users.
  - Providing to shareholders a reasonable return on their investment.
- Provide the general public with information about our activities so that they have a better understanding of our worldwide company.

We believe in contributing to the well-being of the countries and communities where we conduct business, and we commit ourselves to:

- Seek actively the counsel and independent judgement of citizens of each country where we conduct business to provide guidance to local and corporate management, by:

- Selecting independent directors to serve on the board of each of our companies worldwide.
- Retaining distinguished associates and consultants to assist us in conducting our business according to the highest professional standards.

- Contribute to the economic well-being of every country and community where we conduct business, by:
  - Ensuring that new investment fits constructively into the economic development of each host country and local community.
  - Encouraging the use of local suppliers and services offering competitive quality and prices.

- Contribute to the social development of every country and community where we conduct business, by:
  - Providing training programs for the development of skills.
  - Staffing and managing with nationals from those countries wherever practicable.
  - Involving ourselves in social, cultural and educational projects which enhance the quality of life.

- Be a good corporate citizen, by:
  - Complying with and maintaining a due regard for the laws, regulations and traditions of each country where we conduct business.

We believe in improving international understanding, and we commit ourselves to:

- Act with responsible practices in international trade and investment, by:
  - Retaining earnings necessary for reinvestment in our local companies and remitting dividends on a consistent basis.
  - Making royalty, licensing and service agreements which are fair and reasonable and which do not result in any hidden transfer of profits.
  - Limiting foreign exchange transactions to normal business requirements and for the protection of our assets.

- Promote the exchange of ideas and techniques, by:
  - Encouraging the rapid diffusion of new technology to our local companies and licensees, while protecting our ownership rights and investment in such technology.
  - Organising worldwide and regional meetings for the dissemination and exchange of information.
  - Providing support and assistance, especially in technical and professional fields, to develop skills throughout the organisation.
  - Following a balanced approach between transferring people to new jobs to gain experience and leaving people on the job long enough to make positive contributions in their assignments.
  - Participating actively in non-political national and international activities with the objective of improving the global business climate.

The "This We Believe" statement of company philosophy was discussed and ratified by over 200 delegates participating in the Johnson Wax Global Management Conference held in September 1976 in Washington, D.C.

The present text contains refinements introduced into the statement following more than ten years of practising the "This We Believe" business philosophy on a worldwide basis.

## THE WELDON INTERNATIONAL MISSION STATEMENT

*This We Believe*

Quality/Efficiency — Good enough is never good enough

We strive to produce the best product at the best price.

- Editorially
- Pictorially
- In Design
- In Product/ Price
- In Customer Service

*Compassion* — Endeavour to help staff to overcome any personal problems, with help and understanding.

*Honesty* — Our word is our bond. Be prepared for and encourage criticism within and without because we believe that once a hole is identified in our fence, we can fix it.

*Respect and goodwill* — Treat all people with respect and goodwill, our staff equally with our suppliers, our customers, and colleagues.

*Admit your mistakes* — Be open and quick to admit mistakes. Only by mistakes admitted can we move on to success.

*Relationships* — A good deal is good for both parties.

*The environment* — We must always respect the environment and be sensitive to the community in which we work. The community should be proud that we are there.

*Good guests* — Where we work in foreign lands, we must be good guests in that land and respect the local people.

*Strong and aggressive* — People would be naïve if they interpreted our beliefs as a weakness. We are strong and aggressive in protecting our company from bad business.

If any activity, whether in employment, production, or selling, doesn't come within these guidelines, we shouldn't do it.

# Chapter 28

# Some issues of financial management

A contribution from my friend and one-time financial adviser, Simon Gompertz.

Comments and examples in this chapter describe methods used to report fair and relatively true accounting results, assess publishing investments and maintain cash or debt control in a publishing environment. Expenditure and accounting controls have not been covered, as the principles of these do not differ greatly between industries.

## Dangers of deficient accounting

Accrual accounting, though the accepted method of economic appraisal, carries a potential for being wrongly or inadequately applied. The omission of some accruals, the absence of provisions and other value adjustments in line with external realities, and the capitalisation of doubtful assets, can create a very false picture of a result.

Such omissions and commissions, whether politically or commercially fostered, or negligently made by accountants, are the greatest cause of despair among shareholders and their representatives, who faithfully believe in the accuracy of the figures.

Fair economic value accounting will not change the realities. But by reporting them accurately it can avoid the sort of misapprehensions which delude businesses into believing they are making a profit when they are, in fact, making a loss. As I have been quoted elsewhere as saying, it is one thing to suffer a loss, but it is unforgivable to be suffering a loss and think you are making profit. Decisions that flow from such illusions only compound the problem.

Accounting is limited. No-one expects it to be absolute, nor can it remove all subjectivity from the valuation of current assets. Every industry has its statistical history, however, which can be used as a basis for valuing current assets that fail to turn over sufficiently.

## Cash position

Nothing is more important than keeping sight of the cash position. There are many instances of operations reporting large profits, but becoming insolvent (or threatening to) soon after.

Not only is the cash position the net reciprocal effect of every asset, liability and proprietorship item in the balance sheet, but it is also effectively the underbelly of business. Too much cash availability can be inefficient, but too little leaves the business exposed to an excessive interest burden — and possibly much worse.

Any planning exercise must therefore aim to have a cash position that is comfortable, the costs of which are harmonious with the rest of the profit structure.

It is important that we define the "cash position". It is the net sum of:

- Surplus cash on hand or at the bank
- Cash deposits, where amounts can be accessed at any time, whether at a loss of interest or not
- Bank overdrafts and bank loans
- Other loans payable
- Deferred payables of any kind, which by the terms of their original creation are overdue, whether or not interest is payable.

Note that the first two points are usually "positive" figures, while the last two are normally "negative". Some may wish to call this sum net cash or net debt, but I will refer to it simply as cash/debt position.

Some may argue that deferred payables are not a component of a cash/debt position but a "managed" reduction in working capital.

Such an interpretation not only belies the true working capital of the enterprise, but also dangerously misrepresents the cash position (by understatement of a negative component). An undisputed overdue account is a debt; it is no longer an agreed trade credit.

## CASH FORECASTING

When talking about cash forecasting it is important that we separate individual investment activities (activities too small to form a fully-fledged business) from self-contained legal or operating entities, despite their interdependence.

## INDIVIDUAL INVESTMENTS

### Assumptions

Since all business essentially consists of individual activities, it is important that we deal with these first. No investment in any project should be made until a forecast cash flow has been prepared, spelling out the underlying assumptions. These assumptions are much more important than the mechanics of the cash flow exercise. By examining the assumptions the chances of falling short of forecast income can be more readily determined and a contingency plan considered.

While almost all projects lead off with an expense or a commitment to an expense, we expect incomes to exceed any projection of expenditure. Such confidence must be tempered with constant appraisal of the income assumptions so that, if necessary, continuing expenses can be reduced. This mitigation exercise also serves to test the assumptions.

Once under way, the decision to proceed or abandon a project can be based only on the then net of future incomes and future uncommitted expenditures. In other words, costs already incurred or committed will have been sunk and lost. This is why the initial assumptions are so important.

### Methods

The term "cash flow exercise" is used here in the broad sense. It is not absolutely necessary to prepare such flow in the more common "cash book" format. It may be prepared in the profit and loss and balance sheet (PL/BS) form, whereby the cash absorption or generated surplus is implicit in the difference between the assets (excluding cash) and the sum of the liabilities (excluding debt) and the shareholders' funds, including profit to date. This exercise can consolidate a number of approved projects, effectively creating the bulk of the business plan (subject of course to the "backing out" of the imputed costs, if any).

## Imputed costs

There is a tendency to cost into individual projects only those expenses that are charged or identifiable to it. When substantial "energy" is applied from a cost centre (which, from a strict accounting point of view, is counted elsewhere, or from an indirect overhead structure that is considered so fixed that it would continue whether or not the activity took place) that cost must nevertheless be included. The exclusion of such a cost is acceptable only if a transaction is a one-off *and* its commencement and conclusion is virtually concurrent.

In every other case — for the purpose of the evaluation — all costs should be considered, whether they are directly charged or notionally imputed, because in the end energy absorbed by one activity is not available to other activities.

## Discounting for time

When we evaluate a proposed activity, it is important that the periodic cash flows be discounted by a predetermined rate. The rate is based on the cost of money (regardless of whether the project is financed externally or internally) by, say, the overdraft rate for $100 000, plus a profit or risk margin. The margin should be pre-taxed from a post-tax starting point. In other words, if (considering the risk) there is a post-tax required return on investment of 6 per cent and the corporate tax rate is 39 per cent, the pre-tax requirement would amount to approximately 10 per cent. At an overdraft rate of 12 per cent, the total discount rate to be used is 22 per cent. If, by applying this rate, the present value for the whole activity is greater than nil, then the project may proceed.

# OPERATING UNITS

With regard to self-contained operating units, it is more important in cash forecasting to avoid falling below a set cash/debt position in financial terms than it is to forecast accrued profits. Therefore, in spite of potential profits forecast for new activities, the activities may not be approved if current activities combined with these new activities project a cash/debt position below a tolerable pre-set level.

There are ample examples where ignoring a prudent cash position, combined with greed for profits, has had an explosive effect on the whole financial structure and led to the demise of the business, with all its social and ethical consequences.

In order to retain the cash/debt levels, it is vital that a constant forecasting mechanism is in place. Even at its most efficient, conventional accounting can only produce an historical record. What is required is pre-accounting, which reports the balance sheet (and, inferentially, a shortened profit and loss calculation) three individual months in advance of the normal accounting figures. In most cases, the ingredients required for these close estimates are at hand. In a multi-divisional group a consolidation is carried out in the normal way for each of the three projected months.

Comparisons with the original forecast can then be made by using the furthest projected month. If the projected cash position deviates unfavourably and materially from the original plan and forecast, steps can be taken to reduce — either at individual unit levels or at group levels — the amount of cash made available for future activities. Sometime or other, because of timing differences, management will need to make a decision as to whether profit or cash is the priority.

## Charts

I have always strongly believed in the pre-defined and common chart of accounts for multi-divisional business. This enables corporate or group management to understand the meanings of profit and loss and balance sheet headings. Similar businesses within a group can also make prima facie comparisons.

It is true that the master chart has to be broad enough to

accommodate peculiarities of individual divisions. However, unless a group is extremely diverse, the functions are similar. There is a creative stage, a production and manufacturing period, a promotional and sell-in activity and then the order fulfilment and collection time. Through all these stages, divisional management and accounting have a straddling, but separate, function.

## Provisions

The "womb to tomb" cycle of most new publications is two to three years. There is the concept and development stage, the pre-production and manufacturing period, the market preparation and selling time and, finally, the tidying up of inventories and receivables. Cycles for reprints are, of course, shorter. The easiest thing in the world is to give yourself a feeling of profit euphoria during the early part of the cycle, when the possible sting in the tail is naïvely ignored.

By the very nature of book publishing and merchandising, there are pitfalls on the way through. Initially, there is the burden of financing the work in progress. Then there is the importance of the required delivery date, the loss of gross profit on books returned or likely to be returned (sometimes in spite of firm sale arrangements) and, ultimately, the dating or, worse, obsolescence of the book.

These pitfalls mightn't scare an experienced publisher, but they must be recognised in the evaluation and the accounting provisions. Managers who consider themselves above such prudence will eventually pay the penalty.

While allowing for differences in the gestation time of work in progress, in the commercial durability of stocks and in the industry norms of collection delays, there should be (by historical reference) formulas for provisioning against loss of value for all businesses. It is true that formulas are general and may not fit a specific situation. It is also true that if such formulas fit average situations the law-and-order benefits far outweigh the lack of justice in certain individual cases. Managers — and sometimes, by intimidation, their accountants — who are responsible for and are judged by profit or performance, are in most cases not the best people to make subjective assessments of the commercial value of assets at balance sheet closing time.

Obviously each business has its own peculiar "time clock" in respect of the valuation of its assets. History shows what are reasonable formulas, but once they are set no variation should be allowed (except by reference to a higher level of management, and then by a properly rationalised document).

The business manager should realise that a provision is not the end and that realisations can be made in excess of valued down assets, thereby reinstating some profit. There is nothing worse than the boom or bust financial statements of some businesses, resulting from overstated profits and assets in one year and the thud of write-downs the next. Typically, the "good" year can prompt decisions which would not otherwise have been made.

## RETURN ON FUNDS EMPLOYED

Something has already been said about using the present value discounting method to ensure that the return on outlays in a proposed project is no less than minimally required.

For the ongoing concern, the performance measurement must be different, as there is no "cash to cash" cycle for the business as a whole.

I have always relied on the return on "gross funds employed" (GFE) principle, whereby the GFE is the net of all assets and liabilities (other than cash, debt, non-purchased capitalised intangible assets, and income tax items such as provisions, future benefits or prepayments), plus the premium paid for the shares of the business over and above the tangible net asset backing of such shares at the time of purchase.

Ideally, such GFE should be the average of the previous twelve months. But if each month is not available, this can be modified to the average of the last four quarters or the last two six-month periods.

The profit before interest (for example, the net of interest paid and received) and before the write-off of non-purchased intangible assets (if any) and tax expense — known for this purpose as PBIT — for the previous twelve-month period is then taken as a percentage of GFE.

The philosophy in establishing a desirable minimum return is similar to that used for individual projects. As a starting point, an after-tax reward rate is set, pre-taxed and increased, in this case, by a three-year term bond yield. The after-tax risk reward of a business that has some market reputation might be 6 per cent; if such figure is pre-taxed to, say, 9.8 per cent and we add a bond yield of, say, 7 per cent we would get a total of 16.8 per cent. In forecasting, the bond yield at the end of the forecast period may have to be estimated.

This rate of return is merely a desired minimum. The return rates of different divisions can then be compared, as the debt/equity character of each division has been disregarded.

The question might be posed: Why use a financing cost equivalent to an overdraft rate in the case of a new project, when the entire division is judged by a different rate?

The answer is that each new project uses the cost at the end of the financing line, that is, the dearest cost in the spectrum of the division's finance arrangements. In a total business, the underlying cost of money should be the *higher* of the average cost of finance or the bond yield; any return of funds below that would constitute loss.

## FORMS

### Individual projects

As mentioned earlier, in the valuation of an individual project, two methods can be used to arrive at the net cash flows: the cash book method and the PL/BS method.

### Cash book method

This form (see page 153) is based on receipts and expenditure when received and paid for respectively. The line "Other" in expenditure might deal with purchases of equipment or any items not specifically provided for in the stated functional lines.

Imputed costs are expenses (other than interest) which, while not directly charged or allocated to the project, are nonetheless deemed spent in connection with the project.

Whether months or quarters are used is optional, although it is suggested that the periods ("P") should be no less than eight (unless the whole project is shorter) and no more than twenty.

The note column should contain a numerical reference to each of the written assumptions.

The box should contain the Net Present Value (NPV) of the total of the periodical flows, at the discount rate used and indicated. That NPV should be greater than nil.

## PL/BS method

This form (see page 154) is devised for the normal accrual accounting method, where the sales and other incomes are taken up when legally collectable debts arise, and the expense is inserted when incurred. The balance sheet is then filled in, reflecting expense pre-payments and deferments, collection and payment drags, and the cumulative net profit. The net cash flow for each period is then calculated by netting the balance sheet items. The net cash flow shown will be the same as that produced via the Cash Book Method.

This method is somewhat more complex than the cash book method. Its advantage, however, is that, subject to the removal of the imputed costs, it can be used to build up the total business plan or a section of the plan.

The note column should contain a numerical reference to each of the written assumptions.

The box should contain the Net Present Value of the total of the periodical flows, at the discount rate used and indicated. That NPV should be greater than nil.

## The three-months-ahead cash forecast

This form is no more than a slightly rearranged balance sheet, whereby the cash/debt accounts are the equivalent of the remainder of the balance sheet.

Note that to remain within convention (debt is usually seen as a bracketed figure) and to retain adding logic, both liabilities and positive shareholders' funds accounts are shown in brackets.

In the form, column "M0" is the last month for which actual accounts have been prepared; the column marked "Plan M3" should show the figures taken from the active plan and budget and should then be compared with "Forecast M3".

In situations where the containment of the net debt position is critical, this early warning system is vital.

**Project cash flow evaluation — cash book method**

| Project title: | | | | | | | | | | |
|---|---|---|---|---|---|---|---|---|---|---|
| Date prepared: | | | | | | | | | | |
| | Note | NPY | P1 | P2 | P3 | P4 | P5 | P6 | P7 | P8 |
| Receipts | | | | | | | | | | |
| Sales | | | | | | | | | | |
| Other income | | | | | | | | | | |
| Expenditure | | | | | | | | | | |
| (Selling) | | | | | | | | | | |
| (Creative/editorial) | | | | | | | | | | |
| (Pre-production) | | | | | | | | | | |
| (Manufacture/purchase) | | | | | | | | | | |
| (Promotion) | | | | | | | | | | |
| (Distribution) | | | | | | | | | | |
| (Administration) | | | | | | | | | | |
| (Other) | | | | | | | | | | |
| (Imputed costs) | | | | | | | | | | |
| Net surplus (deficit) | | | | | | | | | | |
| Discount rate of % | | | | | | | | | | |

## Project cash flow evaluation — PL/BS method

| | Note | NPY | P1 | P2 | P3 | P4 | P5 | P6 | P7 | P8 |
|---|---|---|---|---|---|---|---|---|---|---|
| Project title: | | | | | | | | | | |
| Date prepared: | | | | | | | | | | |
| Accrued P & L items Revenues | | | | | | | | | | |
| Sales | | | | | | | | | | |
| Other income | | | | | | | | | | |
| Costs | | | | | | | | | | |
| (Selling) | | | | | | | | | | |
| (Creative/editorial) | | | | | | | | | | |
| (Pre-production) | | | | | | | | | | |
| (Manufacture/purchase) | | | | | | | | | | |
| (Promotion) | | | | | | | | | | |
| (Distribution) | | | | | | | | | | |
| (Administration) | | | | | | | | | | |
| (Other) | | | | | | | | | | |
| (Imputed costs) | | | | | | | | | | |
| Net profit (loss) | | | | | | | | | | |
| Net profit (loss) cumulative | | | | | | | | | | |
| Balance sheet | | | | | | | | | | |
| (Prepayments) | | | | | | | | | | |
| (Accounts receivable) | | | | | | | | | | |
| (Work in progress) | | | | | | | | | | |
| (Stocks) | | | | | | | | | | |
| (Fixed assets (net)) | | | | | | | | | | |
| Accounts payable | | | | | | | | | | |
| Accrued expense | | | | | | | | | | |
| Net profit (loss) cumulative | | | | | | | | | | |
| Net balance sheet | | | | | | | | | | |
| Discount rate of % | | | | | | | | | | |

## Three-months-ahead forecast balance sheet

| | Actual M0 | Forecast M1 | Forecast M2 | Forecast M3 | Plan M3 |
|---|---|---|---|---|---|
| Company/Division: | | | | | |
| Date prepared: | | | | | |
| Net cash investment | | | | | |
| Prepayables | | | | | |
| Receivables | | | | | |
| Inventories | | | | | |
| Shares in subs | | | | | |
| Other investments | | | | | |
| Fixed assets (net) | | | | | |
| Intangibles | | | | | |
| (Accrued expense) | | | | | |
| (Payables) | | | | | |
| (Income tax payable) | | | | | |
| (Capital & reserves) | | | | | |
| Retained (profit) loss | | | | | |
| Net | | | | | |
| Cash/debt | | | | | |
| Cash in hand and bank | | | | | |
| Cash deposits | | | | | |
| (Bank overdrafts/loans) | | | | | |
| (Deferred payables) | | | | | |
| Net | | | | | |

# CHAPTER 29

# TRAINING THE NEW GENERATION

*During a crisis we can find funding to produce massive war material and mobilise the youth of the world to fight. Yet we don't seem to regard the unemployed youth of the world as a major crisis in the making.*

**K.E.W.**

Without effective training during the Second World War it would have been impossible to man the tanks, planes and ships pumped out by massive production lines. Without training, the Allies could never have recovered sufficiently in that terrible conflict to eventually defeat the enemy.

The need for training is just as important for business today. This is reflected in the excellent internal and external training programs available worldwide. In my opinion, however, business either selects inappropriate training programs or neglects them altogether. In my experience, management gives too little thought to the real needs of the business when choosing a training scheme. And training for its own sake is pointless. Lazy managers prefer to leave it to the personnel department.

## OTHER VIEWS

Training can be approached at various levels. Firstly, training the people where the action is, the front line, including receptionists, customer relations, retail sales staff and hotel check-ins. Secondly, training the managers and supervisory staff to train the front line people. Thirdly, training people to instruct trainers.

Before starting a training program at any level, identify the real needs of the company:

- Do we need training in the use of new equipment?
- Do we need training in a new technology?
- Do we need to understand our customers' needs?
- Do we need to understand our supplier guidelines/problems?
- Do we need to understand federal, state and municipal regulations?
- Do we need to understand how to conduct business in foreign lands?
- Do we need to learn a new language?
- Do we need to retrain redundant employees?

Programs available for training in all but a few of these areas are nothing short of superb.

## YOUTH TRAINING

As I approach the end of my business career, I am appalled at how economists have convinced the media that the world has no option but to live with high numbers of unemployed. It is totally unacceptable. During a crisis we can find the funding to produce massive war material and mobilise the youth of the world to fight. Yet we don't seem to regard the unemployed youth of the world as a major crisis in the making.

Unemployed, inactive and unfulfilled people, particularly the young, will create huge community problems that will test law and order worldwide. The hooligans we see rioting at soccer matches in Europe are simply unfulfilled youths from areas where up to 30 per cent unemployment has existed for years. The re-emergence in Germany of fascist youth movements is another manifestation of unemployment.

The government must treat unemployment as the most serious problem we will encounter. We must demand visionary leadership that will initiate projects exciting enough to capture young people's imaginations. At least they will maintain a fundamental self-respect if they participate in projects such as the restoration of an historical ship or the rebuilding of old peoples' homes. Just as Kennedy inspired youth with the Peace Corps, we must create jobs to restore their human dignity.

## Companies' responsibility

Every company has a responsibility to train the young for a continuing place in the workforce. Despite my own long commitment, I know I must do more to train young people and open up opportunities for them.

## School-leavers' training scheme

I first acknowledged the trend of school-leavers facing only slender prospects of a worthwhile job when I introduced a school-leavers' training scheme in 1976. From the many applicants we selected seven boys and seven girls to train for twelve months in all aspects of our various companies, from the physical tasks in the warehouse to sales promotion, selling, serving behind counters, direct marketing, financial services and so on.

We first employed a brilliant consultant who, with aptitude tests, accurately predicted what each trainee would best be suited to at the end of their training. For instance, one girl was very good at detailed work and maths; she would have been good in mail order. Another girl had a natural flair for promotion. One boy had artistic talent, and so on. The chosen fourteen were equipped with an attractive uniform with a Hamlyn trainee badge on the blazer, and I persuaded the head of Leyland that his company should lend us fourteen Mini Minors for twelve months for use by the trainees. A Hamlyn Group school-leaver trainee badge we designed was then painted on these cars.

We really put our trainees through all the ropes. Once a month they had to attend a meeting with me and I would give each of them a seemingly impossible challenge. They might have to use their initiative to spend a week in the field with current affairs anchorman Mike Willesee, or spend a week with the head of Westpac bank. Pleasingly, they were able to meet these challenges, largely because the people at the top enjoyed encouraging young people.

*The Hamlyn trainee's badge.*

Were there any problems? Only those caused by internal politics. Divisional managers resented having these young kids commenting on their operations. I remember one division they reported on: they thought the manager's office upstairs was palatial, with all the latest furniture and beautiful carpet, while the retail outlet downstairs was untidy at best. When the manager explained that they were moving out of the building in six months, a young school-leaver shot back, "That might be so, but there is no excuse for filthy toilets!" Ah, the fearless honesty of youth!

Another criticism from my managers was that the good trainees would inevitably leave. The project was therefore a waste of money, they said. My response was that, to my knowledge, no-one was actually trained by the book publishing industry. We just stole qualified people from each other to suit our purposes at the time. If we trained more people, I argued, the industry as a whole would benefit. In my opinion, too many companies refuse to train people, simply because they fear they might end up working for somebody else.

The other major criticism was that we had formed an elitist group. As it happens, I'm all for building up an elitist group of people. If an elitist group achieves because they work as one and if being elitist makes you look good and feel like a winner, let's all aim for an elitist team, because you are talking quality.

I recall suggesting to Neal Blewett, the then Minister for Trade, that we should halve the personal tax rate of all sales people who sold product overseas. "That would create an elitist group," he replied, in a tone indicating disapproval. Can you imagine how totally focused on exports Australia would be if our training and rewards encouraged an elitist group of global sales people?

It's fair to claim that those school-leavers our company trained in 1976 have all done well, or better than might otherwise have been expected. At the time of writing they must be approaching their mid-thirties. I don't know where they all are now, but one is a producer with "60 Minutes", another is a manager of a book/direct marketing company, another is an art director and one edits a magazine. Though some stayed on at Weldons for some time, I encouraged them to leave the nest and find their own way.

In the context of the profit we made in the group at the time, the cost of training was negligible. It contributed greatly to the trainees' self-esteem and, in a small way, sent a positive signal to the nation's youth.

It also contributed to our own self-esteem, might I say.

# CHAPTER 30

# OUTSIDE INTERESTS ARE NO HINDRANCE TO BUSINESS

I borrowed money from the bank to build a new clubhouse,
and then organised the sale of chooks at hotels
to pay off the debt.

**K.E.W.**

Scratch the surface of a number of businessmen and you will find an ex-lifesaver, footballer, cricketer, or church-worker underneath. I have found, in the main, that business is easier to conduct with sports people and that there is a national network once you discover it.

In my case, I owe much of my success to my activities in the lifesaving movement. I joined Pacific Surf Club as a fifteen-year-old cadet during the 1948–49 season, while still at Brisbane Grammar School. The club had only been founded the year before by much older chaps, some in their mid-twenties and thirties. Imagine a young lad being thrown in with forty men — eating, sleeping and surfing together. I was very fortunate indeed. I had the rough edges knocked off me very quickly and soon learned that I had to stand up for myself or get the hell belted out of me. The men who are still around from this period are very special to me, and to this day I meet many of them over the Christmas period.

At the age of sixteen I became social organiser of the club. I organised open air pictures on the beach with old Charlie Chaplin films. I organised dances at the Norman Park RSL Hall, travelling by train to Sandgate to get the crabs and prawns for supper. I was thrilled by this freedom and responsibility.

I built an exciting young team around me and we raised money as I went on through the club to become vice-captain, captain and then chief instructor. I ran midnight-to-dawn dances, borrowed money from the bank to build a new clubhouse, and then organised the sale of chooks through hotels to pay off the debt.

I eventually became president of the club, and like to think we built it up into one of the best clubhouses in the state. Not only did we own it, but we also owned lots of land around it. In fact, while still a trustee of the club and living in Sydney, I noticed the club had stopped selling chooks at the Palm Beach Hotel. When I asked a member why, he said they had paid everything off. So I got the two other trustees and we bought more land next door, putting them into debt again. They soon paid this off.

This authority to make decisions on raising funds and constructing buildings at such a young age provided me with wonderful training and the expertise to fulfil some of my little visions. It also taught me the value of comradeship and emphasised the tenuous grip we have on life. My best friend, Des Quinlan, was taken by a shark near me in 1952, and another very dear friend, Tony Laracy, drowned when he was captain of the club and I was president. I could see nothing but tragedy in these two events, until I came to realise that the inner strength I had to find to deal with these tragedies later enabled me to cope with personal and business crises when they arose.

In 1970, having been the Queensland delegate to the National Council of Surf Lifesaving, I was approached to form an international lifesaving group. Though honoured, I accepted only on the proviso that it would be truly international, with the headquarters moved around the world. This experience taught me much that helped my business career, because I had to bring together Americans, Australians, New Zealanders, British, South Africans, Sri Lankans, Indonesians and, towards the end, many people from European countries.

During this exercise I learnt that some countries believed that everything they did was best. Our people certainly felt Australia was pre-eminent in the lifesaving movement in the early 1970s. To the contrary, our equipment was so out of date that it was next to useless.

*The author addresses the Huntington Beach Lifeguard's dinner in California in 1974 as the President of the World Lifesaving movement he founded.*

Eventually we brought the countries together for educational conferences, complete with their equipment and medical advisers. I am proud to say the organisation I founded was responsible for a dramatic change in lifesaving techniques and equipment worldwide. The Australian surfer owes the protection offered by the Westpac helicopter rescue service to a technique developed by the Auckland branch of surf lifesaving in New Zealand. The "rubber ducky", or inshore rescue boat, was first developed by a Commander Thompson of Atlantic College in Cornwall, England, and further refined by an Australian, Harry Brown. It rescues more people in Australia than anything else.

Then there was the Torpedo Tube, developed by US lifeguards in 1930. When arguing at one meeting about the relative merits of the reel-in line and the Torpedo Tube, one world-weary Australian official spoke up: "What could those Yanks tell us?".

"And how many people have you rescued?" I asked.

"Two in 1949," he said firmly.

I explained that I had seen 600 people rescued in three days with the tube at Huntington Beach in California! (Don't we come across similarly closed minds in business?) Case closed.

World Lifesaving is in the process of being enlarged to include about seventy countries. Between them they account for about 180 000 rescues each year. Apart from the pride I take in having helped establish it, the organisation has equipped me with a great knowledge of handling people of all nationalities. Needless to say, that knowledge has been invaluable in business.

It is easy to see, then, why I have always encouraged managers to take on outside activities. Our lives should never be confined to business alone. By pursuing an outside interest, we can build up contacts with totally different people and discuss broader issues that might put a new perspective on some business problem. And if that doesn't seem enough of a reason, I truly believe that all work and no play makes Jack a very dull boy.

# CHAPTER 31

# PROFILES

Each one of these marvellous characters has in some way
shaped my business career.

**K.E.W.**

# Bill Hanna

*Yabbadabbadoo!*

I first met Bill in the early 1970s. He was the most gentle, loving
person I'd ever met in business. No wonder! He was the creator of
all my favourite cartoon characters, from Tom and Jerry to Fred
Flintstone and Yogi Bear. With Joe Barbera, he created all the
marvellous Hanna Barbera characters.

One day Bill approached me, explaining that his new owner was
anxious to find an Australian partner to animate cartoons in
Australia for the American Saturday TV Network cartoon segment.
We decided to give it a go at Hamlyn, and formed a joint venture
known as Hanna Barbera Australia. It went on to produce live
action documentaries and became a very profitable division of the
Hamlyn Group.

Despite this great man's status, when setting up the company he
would fly out to Australia, personally buy timber from the yard,
and build all the animation desks — in a parking lot under the
building! Having made the desks, he would sit with all these young
kids, patiently teaching them the techniques of animation. He
would also spend time with them after business hours, always
offering genuine encouragement.

One of the main reasons for Hanna Barbera's success was the preparedness of this living legend of animation to give so much of his talent and time to the young. I recently had a reunion with Bill and the original team of Sam Johnson, Dudley Taft and Neil Balnaves, at Bill's fishing lodge in California. Bill, who had already had his second bypass operation, was rushing off to Korea at the age of eighty-three to teach young people animation! I'm honoured to say I've known him and worked with him. His inspirational message is that, no matter how old you are, you can have a role in business imparting knowledge to the young.

# Dan Grenville

*He gave untried and unproven young people a go —*
*and they succeeded!*

This man made a big impact on the book trade in Australia in the 1950s by importing paperbacks and merchandising them in revolving stands to the mass market in all kinds of new outlets. He also started mail order companies and the first budget record business in Australia (which I later bought for the Hamlyn Group).

Dan gave me my first management job, establishing a Queensland branch in the late 1950s. There is a funny story leading up to this advancement, from when I was still a sales rep for N.S. Pixley & Sons, which represented Grenville's book agencies in Brisbane.

One Friday, Dan asked me to meet him at Coolangatta airport and spend the weekend at the new Chevron Hotel. We discussed book business in the afternoon, had dinner, and moved on to the hotel nightclub. We had enjoyed quite a few drinks when a beautiful singer came on to sing a few brackets. When she returned to her seat, Dan said, "Kevin, why don't you ask her for a dance?" Believing that Dan was testing my get-up-and-go, I pranced over to ask her.

"No thanks," she replied in a deep, silky voice, "and bugger off!"

At midnight Dan challenged me to try again — and not to take "no" for an answer! This time I was not going to be put off. I strode over determinedly to where she was sitting and asked again. This time she knew I was serious. "Yes," she said.

Well, I felt a million dollars. I had succeeded and Dan would be dazzled. I gave him a cocky look as I danced past his table.

When I sat down half an hour later, the glamorous singer performed the finale of her act, stripping down to a G-string. "She" was a female impersonator! If only the floor could have opened up and swallowed me. Everyone seemed to be staring at me. Dan claimed he hadn't known. At least he appointed me Queensland manager the following day.

Dan died, aged seventy-eight, in August, 1992. He was a man who never hesitated to give eighteen to twenty-year-olds a chance to make it in management. He was positive, kind, visionary, fair, hard-working and loyal to his staff. He is hardly remembered today, but the businesses he initiated in the 1950s still flourish, and the people who run them readily acknowledge his wonderful leadership and vision. His epitaph should read: "He gave untried and unproven young people a go — and they succeeded!"

# Fred Smith

*He had a wonderful ability to make you feel part of a team.*

I met Fred Smith when he was managing director of K.G. Murray Publishing Company, founded by Ken Murray. Then publisher of *Man* magazine, Ken Murray went on to establish the first commercial ski resorts at Perisher Valley, installing ski lifts and building three hotels. K.G. Murray was a publicly-listed company in the early 1960s, though the majority of shares were held by the Murray family. When K.G. Murray acquired Greenseas Tuna, that company had just sold its fish-canning activities to Kraft and had £1 million cash in the bank from the sale. Greenseas also had a subsidiary book distribution company called Grenville Publishing Company, for which I was national sales manager. But Fred Smith was not interested in Grenville. His sights were set on the cash.

After the acquisition, the Cuffe family, which had owned Greenseas, retired and Fred appointed me general manager of Grenville. K.G. Murray was highly profitable at this time and one of the largest magazine companies in Australia. Its magazines were distributed by Gordon & Gotch under the supervision and direction of a circulation manager called Doug Spicer. K.G. Murray's success in magazines was in no small part due to its impeccable attention to the sales records of each newsagent.

Fred was then a mature gentleman in his sixties with amazing physical and mental energy. He would run up the stairs of our six-storey building, rush into your office and demand, "What's doing here?" He was also the most frugal managing director I have ever met in my life. No-one in my business career has ever come close to matching him.

Particularly mean with company cars, he'd make you drive the same one for five years and give you a right royal blast if you spent any money on repairs or maintenance. We thought we were badly done by until the day a taxi driver boasted to Fred that his cab had turned over 250 000 miles. Fred immediately dictated that all company cars had to be driven for 200 000 miles before replacement, generously conceding the odd 50 000 miles.

One day, the brakes failed on my clapped-out company car while driving down the ramp of a city parking station. I ran it up onto a railing, abandoned it, and raced up to see Fred. I told him that his f— car had crashed and that I would put my life at risk no longer. The next day my immediate boss, Doug Spicer, was told to buy a new company car and to hand down his old one. So, I still didn't get a new car!

I guess Fred must have influenced my attitude to company cars, because I was more generous than most employers over the years. More significantly, Fred had the ability to get employees together for drinks at the local pub. He had a wonderful ability to make you feel part of a team. I enjoyed a long relationship with Fred and, until his death, Fred would occasionally pop up at functions I put on. He believed he had contributed to my learning curve — and so he had, the mean, lovable old bastard.

# Horrie Hogarth

*Listen, son, good enough is never good enough.*

Horrie Hogarth was in charge of the *Truth* newspaper process-engraving department in Brisbane, Queensland, when I was an apprentice half-tone etcher in the 1950s. The department had a reputation for the best letterpress engraving in Australia, particularly its colour work. Horrie was very much the master to my apprentice and, more than any other person, he taught me two things: never compromise on quality, and allow workers time with the boss now and then to express their feelings — including why he's a lousy boss!

Horrie was a tough customer, but occasionally, quite out of the blue, he would offer to buy a drink on the *Truth*. He would gather us all around — foreman, journeymen, and older apprentices — and quite a few drinks would be enjoyed while work problems were discussed. There would be suggestions on how we might improve and where the company might be doing the wrong thing. It could get heated at times, but Horrie gave us the chance to get frustrations off our chest. Nothing much changed, but at least we felt better. More importantly, it made us feel part of a team.

In those days a double-page spread in letterpress for, say, a rose catalogue could take two weeks to finish and proof. Horrie would reject, say, the yellow plate, which might take a week to re-make. If the craftsman complained, Horrie would say, "Listen, son, good enough is *never* good enough. Haven't you noticed how we pay higher wages, plus overtime? You notice we don't have sales reps trying to find business? The fact is, we still attract an enormous amount of colour work *because* the trade knows it gets the best work here. If I allowed 'good enough' to be good enough, it wouldn't be long before the standard was definitely *not* good enough."

He wouldn't compromise on quality, relative to price, and his customers kept returning. His attitude stuck in your mind.

I was indeed a lucky young man to have worked with Horrie Hogarth and his team in that department. I regarded them then, and I consider them still, the best I could have worked with. They gave me a sound grounding for my life ahead and taught me what a real work situation was all about.

# Lloyd O'Neil

*Lloyd inspired me by going out on his own at a difficult time
and fulfilling some of his big visions.*

I first met Lloyd O'Neil in the late 1950s when he worked with
Brian Clouston, the founder of Jacaranda Press. Later, Lloyd
established the Lansdowne Press in Melbourne before selling out to
Frank Cheshire, then the largest educational publisher in Australia.

Lloyd eventually headed up the whole Cheshire Group. When he
left after a disagreement he founded Curry O'Neil Publishing and,
more significantly, the visionary Rigby Reading and Maths
Programs. These were to evolve into the enormously successful
educational product that brought Weldon so much business in the
USA. Lloyd developed these projects with John Gilder and Sue
Donovan, brilliant people who are now my associates and partners.

Lloyd was gentle and shy beneath what seemed at times an aloof,
businesslike manner. He was always keen to learn the finer points
of running a business and would contact me for advice because (I
guess) he wrongly believed I had been formally trained in the
business aspects of publishing and marketing.

It was Lloyd O'Neil who really pulled me out of the bunch by
identifying me to Paul Hamlyn.

Our relationship began when we were both given the chance to
attend the Frankfurt Book Fair in 1968, the first overseas trip for
either of us. I was somewhat isolated at the fair because K.G.
Murray was not a member of the Book Publishers' Association of
Australia. Quite reasonably, I was not allowed on their stand, so I
was forced to wander around as a maverick, selling well and
finding exciting new agencies. As Lloyd watched me he became
embarrassed that an Australian group would keep one of their kind
out in the cold, so he invited me in.

When the fair was over, I put an irresistible idea to him. "My
boss wants to know my every move and every cent I spend," I said.
"But I'm not leaving Europe until I see Paris. Why don't we play
hooky for three days and drive there?" Diligent and proper as Lloyd
was, he eventually weakened.

We had a grand time, talking endlessly about Australian book publishing and how we could perform as well as any foreign publishers. We swapped ideas, enthusiasm and yarns, forging a long-lasting relationship of mutual respect. Though we later became fierce competitors, unknown to others we kept in regular contact and exchanged advice.

Lloyd was later struck by a dreadful cancer and I was honoured to be part of a retrospective of his publishing. Lloyd had inspired me by going out on his own at a difficult time and fulfilling some of his big visions. It was in part his encouragement which enabled me to find the guts to leave the Hamlyn Group and have a go.

# Lyn Holloway

*Lyn Holloway had the greatest courage in the world to back an individual Australian.*

I first met expatriate Australian Lyn Holloway when I was doing business with the Straits Times Press publishing and printing conglomerate in Singapore. A very friendly man (and great golfer), he was involved in various top marketing roles, generating enormous revenue for the newspapers.

A few years after I met him, the chief executive of the company, Bill Simmons, retired and Lyn replaced him. We continued to work together, Straits Times printing and selling a number of our books.

When I went out on my own, Lyn suggested we might do something together. At the time I was really browned off with the corporate scene, having learned that the so-called heads of operations, when it came down to it, either didn't have the guts to make decisions or passed the buck to head office or the parent board. Accordingly, my response to this generous offer was arrogant and to the point.

"Sorry, Lyn, but I don't think that any of you guys running corporations have much power at all. When you deposit $1 million in a bank account in Australia, then I'll believe you've got authority. I don't know what the hell I'm going to do at this stage, but if you want to back me this will really test your clout."

To my astonishment, after some hesitation from his financial director, $1 million arrived in Australia. Far from being gratified, I was terrified! I didn't want to touch it!

In the end these funds were properly documented and held in a bank account I never touched. The activities I created didn't require the money and it was eventually returned, with interest. Lyn's show of faith earned him some extra dividends because of the successful people I introduced him to. Lyn Holloway had the greatest courage in the world to back an individual Australian. His bold gesture remains very special to me.

Tom McIlwain, Lyn's brilliant financial man, also supported me and played a big part in our joint successes. He could write an agreement during discussions, never missing the finest detail. And when Lyn and I got excited about a deal, Tom would arrange the finance with a speed unknown in big corporations in those days. The three of us put enormous energy into the takeover of Marshall Cavendish. I'm proud to say that through Lyn's great faith in me, and because he is one of the greatest publishers I have known (he *thinks* like a publisher), Straits Times more than doubled its earnings within two years under his leadership. From making money in Singapore, the company began to make as much again offshore in the UK.

When Lyn Holloway retired from Straits Times, Rupert Murdoch identified him as the man with the greatest knowledge of newspapers and publishing in the East. I may be wrong, but Lyn knew a great deal about the *South China Morning Post* when Murdoch employed him in a roving consultancy role. I feel certain that when Murdoch took over that journal and quadrupled its profits, Lyn would have had a lot to do with identifying its growth potential.

A great publisher he may be, but I would be negligent if I didn't mention that he was *always* late for appointments, with the excuse that he had been delayed by some exciting political or business development. Lyn's lack of punctuality notwithstanding, Rupert Murdoch is very lucky to have him around.

Lyn Holloway inspired me to identify a winner, back him, and then leave him alone to get on with it.

# Lord (Don) Ryder

*I would like to think that we have spent $900 000*
*to teach you how to run a business, Kevin.*

When I met Don Ryder, he was the head of the Reed Paper Group in England, then 25 per cent owned by Hamlyn's parent company, the International Publishing Corporation (IPC). I had been asked to show him our new premises at Hamlyn and generally entertain him during a Sydney visit.

The following year Cecil King, the power in IPC, was deposed in a boardroom coup by Hugh Cudlip. Shortly afterwards Don Ryder made a reverse takeover of IPC, which suddenly found itself a subsidiary of Reed International. Ryder was now the boss.

Ryder would visit all the international offices to receive the business plans for the following year. My own presentation was going to be a disaster: I had allowed two divisional managers to make some major mistakes and my results were going to be nearly $1 million down on projections. My immediate superiors were expressing their dissatisfaction with these results to the chief in their preamble to my presentation, when Ryder stopped them in their tracks.

"Just a moment," he said, "what you're telling me is the past. Kevin made $900 000 less than he should have, but I want to hear no more about the past. We can't do anything about it, but we can sure as hell do something about the future. "I would like to think that we have spent $900 000 to teach you how to run a business, Kevin. In the context of the world group, we can afford it. It's not a lot of money, because I know you are going to do very well next year."

Imagine my astonishment! I had expected him to sack me. To the contrary, in one fell swoop he gave me the confidence to rebound from a mistake and move on to success. The following year we returned huge profits.

Since that day I have told up-and-coming executives who have made costly mistakes that the money need not be wasted if it teaches them how to manage a business. It is Don Ryder's legacy.

Ryder had presence. When he walked into a room you knew who was boss. He didn't endear himself to a lot of people, and I suspect he took too much advice from his so-called specialists. Philip Jarvis, then chief executive of the UK Hamlyn Group, resigned rather than work for him. Nevertheless, I'm forever grateful to him for having shown me that forgiving genuine mistakes can encourage managers to achieve better things.

# Vivian Weldon, my father

*I learnt a lot about human nature from my father.*
*First and foremost, I valued his ability to mix freely*
*with all levels of society.*

My father was one of five children — four brothers and a sister — raised in the maritime suburb of Balmain, in Sydney's inner west. His father (also Vivian) was one of thirteen Weldons born on Goat Island in Sydney Harbour. My great grandfather, William Weldon, was the foreman in charge of the colony's powder magazine on the island.

My grandfather rose through the marine ranks from grease monkey to engineer to skipper, serving on every ferry owned by the Sydney Ferry Company. He was skipper of the showboat *Kalang* when he retired.

My father served his apprenticeship and time as a fitter and turner at Cockatoo Island Dockyard, and later worked as a marine engineer. Like my uncles, he became an engineer in coastal shipping.

In 1916, he volunteered for the Australian Flying Corps, serving at Laverton and Point Cook in Victoria until the end of the First World War. His first solo flight was on a Pusher Fairman. In the few hours of that flight he carried off a fence, ripped the wheels and skids from the plane and then, being an engineer, proceeded to repair the damage. My father feared nothing in life; he would have a go at anything.

After the war he continued to work as an engineer on coastal shipping along the east coast of Australia. However, after meeting my mother in Brisbane, he decided to become a landlubber, opening a small cleaner and disinfectant business in Brisbane's Fortitude Valley. There he developed a technique to solidify phenyl, blocks of which were hung to freshen dunnies in the 1930s and 1940s. His retail outlet also supplied industrial soaps and the like. But, as with so many in those dark years, he went broke during the Depression.

*The author with his father at the Ingham Show, Queensland, 1939.*

He had four children to feed (and I was on the way), so he bought a load of brushes and brooms and headed north on a train, hopping on and off to sell his wares. He was the world's most optimistic salesman. As far as he was concerned, anything he sold was of the best quality on earth. Nevertheless, when he spotted an advertisement for an engineer at Inkerman Mill, Ayr Home Hill, near Ingham, the whole family moved north in the mid-1930s.

When he left the mill he formed a motor business with a man called Eric Hobbs. Hobbs & Lukeidge later became Weldon & Hobbs and then Weldon Motors, holders of the Ford franchise for the north of Queensland. He also had the agency for the Radiola short-wave radio.

When I returned to Ingham after an absence of thirty-five years I met "Smacka" Carr, who had worked with my father. He told me a story which typified my father's way of doing business. In the late 1930s Ingham's population was mainly Italian sugar cane farmers, many of whom became great friends with my father. They were fascinated by Mussolini's rise to power in Italy, particularly his emotional, melodramatic speeches. According to Smacka, to demonstrate the wireless to the Italian farmers my father would scale a local church spire and attach the Radiola aerial. Then, twisting the knob of the Radiola, he would mutter, "Speak, Mussolini, you bastard, speak!" Any snippet from Mussolini would guarantee an instant sale and more profit than he would make on a Ford motor car!

The motor trade remained his main business, however. I remember him telling me that once he sold a new model Ford to one sugar cane farmer, the rest was relatively easy. If he sold a car to Giovanni then, when he drove out of the gate and along the long road of sugar cane, the next farmer would already be waiting at his gate:

"You sold Giovanni a new Ford?"

"My word!" said my father.

"Okay. I buy too?"

Once he had secured the first deal, he would close an order for ten. He taught me that once the first sale was locked away, the momentum was in train. He didn't believe in scattering your energies. Just concentrate hard on that first sale. It is human nature that once somebody else makes the initial commitment, others find it easier to follow.

Vivian Weldon was the first man to drive a motor car in towns like Tully, in north Queensland. He would travel far and wide on dirt tracks while selling and, if he arrived late, accommodation could be very scarce in those small country towns. It was nothing for four salesmen to share a room in those days, even two in a double bed. "If you were late," said my father, "you had to climb in beside a bloke already asleep. It was hell, because he was often pie-eyed and snoring like the devil." My father's technique was to run his hand up the other bloke's leg, which would wake him with a start — and, while he watched my father suspiciously all night, keeping as far apart as he could, my father would sleep soundly in the additional space and blessed silence.

My father threw himself into the Italian community. For years his best friend was Peter Musso, founder of Australia's first spaghetti company. Father was a great cook himself, particularly of Italian cuisine. (He showed me that a man can cook well and should find the preparation of food interesting.) He loved making his own sausages, and pressed tongue with an elaborate press system of his own design.

I guess I learnt a lot about social interaction from my father, particularly the ability to mix freely without regard for wealth or position. A smooth old gentleman in his way, he also taught me to respect women. He got into a lot of fights in his time ensuring others behaved with suitable propriety in their presence.

He appeared to me to be unconsciously brave. When the Second World War came, he was on his way to Flinders Naval Depot within six hours. (My poor mother had to sell the business, auction everything and drag her five kids to live in Brisbane.) Father started as chief engineer of a minesweeper, then moved on to a confiscated China trading ship, the *Po Yang*. The *Po Yang* supplied ammunition for the Allied bombardments, from New Guinea to the final great sea battle at Laeyte Gulf. He attended the Japanese surrender in Ambon. I often thought how brave he was to be locked away every two weeks in the engine room of a ship packed with high explosives, steaming through enemy waters to some new theatre of war.

During the war years he made model boats, took photographs and, in one cherished memory, traded a case of Scotch whisky for a brand new diesel landing-craft for the ship. He was making deals and having fun. He appeared to think the war was one great, adventurous hoot and seemed disappointed when it ended. What I learned from him was his positive attitude to a difficult job, with never a whinge. Obviously he'd learned from *his* father, because I remember Dick, as Dad called him, saying, "You've got to put more into the job than the job requires. Then you'll get more enjoyment from it. I'm paid to skipper this ship from A to B on the harbour. But on the way I make the passengers aware of the other passing passenger ships, give them a bit of history about the harbour, explain how the ship's propelled and how the lifesaving equipment works."

In short, he put more into his job and got more out of it. It was an attitude he passed to his son, and his son passed it on to me.

After the war my father started a business for woodworking, machinery and anything else he could get his hands on that he thought would sell. He sold thousands of what I think were called Quickway Mop Buckets, a bucket fitted with two rollers to wring out the mop when you stood on a foot pedal.

My mother died suddenly, aged forty-eight, when I was seventeen. Dad eventually started a restaurant on the Gold Coast. (Another major lesson I learned from my father was never, but *never*, open a restaurant.) When he remarried a much younger woman at the age of sixty he fathered two more children. He showed me that, no matter what your age, you can do almost anything if you remain positive. He died in 1982, aged eighty.

My father was no angel. He was a tough disciplinarian and, like his own father, could blow a fuse very easily. But he was always ready for a new adventure, and when people greeted him he'd respond with: "I feel wonderful! I'm excited! I woke up this morning!"

Start each day with an exciting outlook, a sense of fun, and be grateful you are alive. That's the positive attitude he passed on to me. It has helped me in business and in life.

# Paul Hamlyn

*... he stormed the world, selling to people
who had never bought books before.*

The man who most influenced me to take a fresh approach to book publishing was the Englishman, Paul Hamlyn. I doubt that anybody in the past 100 years of book publishing has accumulated such a large personal fortune from this industry.

Paul Hamlyn entered publishing by buying the rights to reprint and republish books traditional publishers could not sell. He shrewdly identified *why* they hadn't sold and then corrected the flaws. They might have been too expensive, unimaginatively titled, not bulky enough or labouring under a poor jacket design. With his then wife Bobby he sold the reprints under the Books for Pleasure imprint. He ultimately produced his own books and personally sold each product to the main accounts throughout England, USA and Australia. He employed Philip Jarvis as chief executive and together they continued the imprint's creative output.

By the mid-1960s, Paul Hamlyn books stood out in the bookshops like no others because of their appealing presentation and exceptional value. They were marketed aggressively and successfully. It was at this point that Philip Jarvis phrased the memorable question "Why shouldn't books be sold in supermarkets like soap?" Traditional British publishers were aghast, but comforted themselves that this young upstart, Hamlyn, would never last ...

Of course, Paul Hamlyn stormed the world, selling to people who had never bought books before. Hamlyn exploited high traffic areas, impulse buying and all the modern marketing techniques the book world had studiously ignored. Prior to Paul Hamlyn, a book sold only if somebody walked into a bookshop and asked for a title by its subject heading — natural history, art, gardening and so on.

His international success was so sensational that he attracted the attention of Cecil King, then head of IPC, one of the largest newspaper, magazine and book-publishing companies in the world. It owned the very old and established *Odhams, Newnes,*

*Illife*, and *Country Life*. King felt that by acquiring Hamlyn he would lift IPC's rather antiquated book companies into the twentieth century. So, Paul Hamlyn sold out at forty to become a multi-millionaire and part of IPC. The bright people who had worked beside him also did well because of his generosity.

The next five years were very tense for Paul and his management. Saddled with the corporate mentality, Paul had all the fun and direction squeezed out of him. He was hamstrung by boardroom battles, inefficient computerisation, and distribution systems designed for the benefit of newspaper unions. When his contract finished, he left.

Back in 1960 it was all very different. It was Paul's happiest time. With his unorthodox approach to business, he genuinely believed that people working with him should have fun. Even rarer in those days, he gave graduates direct from university a chance in publishing.

I remember one, Joan Clibbon, fresh from university, throwing herself into producing one of Paul Hamlyn's biggest bestsellers, *Cookery in Colour*. It sold 100 000 copies in its first year. Having sold out in the UK, Hamlyn decided to establish a presence in Australia. I was hardly known to him, but as I had recommendations from the likes of Lloyd O'Neil he approached me to establish the Paul Hamlyn Group in Australia.

The ink had hardly dried on the deal before he said, "I want you to come to England and put your plan to our new owners. You must bring your wife. We will make a special apartment available, with a maid, to ensure she is able to discover the delights of London while you work."

I couldn't believe it. I remember telling my wife, Glenda, that it was too good to be true and that there had to be a catch. There was no catch. It made an ordinary Queensland boy feel very special and talented. Otherwise, why would such a man waste his money on me? With that one generous gesture he instilled in me enough confidence to really believe I was going to accomplish the dream of dreams that had been floating around in my mind. From that moment on I knew I would build the most successful and innovative publishing organisation in Australia.

It didn't stop there, either. When I got to England I was invited to informal dinners with all the directors of IPC — the Cudlips, the Gordon Cartwrights and Ellis Bourkes, people who were among the most notable in the publishing business at the time. It was pretty heady stuff.

Paul delegated skilfully. After accepting my vision for the Australian group in principle — it happily mirrored his own — he sent me to the IPC group financial controller, Eddie Weiss, to explain the funding required. With considerable apprehension I asked for $1 million, half in capital and half in loan funds. Eddie Weiss finally looked up. "Well," he said, "that's not very much money, is it?"

I still have a copy of the $1 million cheque because it had to be made out to me first, with a quick back-to-back cheque from me to a new company account.

With Paul's support I began building at Dee Why what was to be the most functional and attractive publishing complex in Australia. Though on the outskirts of Sydney, it had the latest warehousing equipment, landscaped grounds, swimming pools ... the lot. We hit the ground running so hard that we experienced enormous success in a very short period. Though Paul was continually harassed by the specialists at his head office who thought I'd gone too troppo for anything to really work, he never once pulled me back. In fact, he kept many of his advisors at bay by countermanding their instructions.

His timing in establishing the company in Australia was absolutely perfect. And his timing in approaching me was absolutely perfect, ready as I was to produce his style of books about Australia, for Australians.

We worked intensely during our brief time together in Australia, and, although Paul was very demanding in terms of hours, we always had lots of laughs.

Paul was an incredible salesperson, with an ability to mesmerise a client with naked enthusiasm and assurances of how the product would benefit everyone. With the client firmly in the palm of his hand, he would close the deal with exquisite timing.

*The author with Paul Hamlyn in 1968. The Australian publishing scene was about to be shaken to its roots.*

I recall when he had the chairman of EMI visit the Marlene Dietrich suite he always took at the Old Australia Hotel. He wanted to convince the man that he should give us EMI's repertoire for a budget music company we planned to start in Australia. (Paul had just done the same thing in England with Music For Pleasure.)

Paul was in the middle of the most dramatic sales pitch I had ever seen when I eventually caught his eye to point out that the dear old chairman was fast asleep. Paul jumped up and clapped his hands, "Kevin! Kevin! Open the windows and let some air in this bloody room!" The chairman woke up, startled and embarrassed. Paul instantly popped the question and the deal was done. EMI agreed to give us the repertoire and press our records.

It proved that even when things look really bad, you should be prepared to risk something really dramatic to pull the deal out of oblivion.

On another occasion Paul and I were invited to a board luncheon of one of Australia's largest insurance companies. He sat next to the chairman, who was the most boring, dissipated Australian you would never want to meet. He kept talking about the war, although Paul couldn't follow which particular war he had in mind. I overheard him tell Paul that he was chairman of twenty-eight companies and he was thinking of giving some of them up.

Paul then leaned across to me and whispered, "Kevin, he's *thinking* of giving them up!" It was further evidence that, despite the existence of some elderly directors who are vigorous and imaginative, there are others who are hopeless and should be removed.

Paul always insisted that the work environment be attractive and different, something I have tried to emulate. And he always travelled well, with considerable style. He was never picky about how you entertained or how you travelled, provided you landed the order. But he would drive you mad if you were spending the money without achieving the sales.

Paul remains a man whose mannerisms, dress and methods are infectious. Some people who worked with him became more Paul than Paul. He always thought me a rather down-to-earth, rough Australian, but now and again even I find myself "doing a Paul". Like forcing the caller to ramble on the telephone by making no response, or not being too anxious to do all the talking when it's a business deal. I have copied many of his successful ideas, particularly in employing women in management when others wouldn't have dreamed of it.

How very lucky I have been to have had Paul as my friend and mentor, as much today as ever. And his timing is still perfect.

# Peter Owen

*Peter stood tall as one of the brightest new people in
the newspaper industry in his time — a visionary ...*

When I first met Peter, he had been head-hunted from a
management consultancy group after conducting a study of the
*Adelaide Advertiser* newspaper group. Appointed chief executive of
the group, he immediately launched an aggressive acquisition and
development program.

His intelligence and energy astonished me. Having displayed the
vision to set up the first computer data processing company in
Australia for the group, he promptly acquired Australia's largest
printing works, Wilkie and Co. With lieutenants like Brian Price,
he reinvigorated the group's floundering printing interests with a
new plant and sophisticated technology. He transformed a small,
local newspaper into a highly profitable national printing and
publishing conglomerate in a very short time.

One of his strong suits was an ability to quickly absorb the
complexities of new businesses. His comprehension of the new
technology sweeping the information and printing industries was
remarkable. Old newspaper lags and journos soon learned that he
couldn't be hoodwinked.

There was a real bond between us. For my part, I felt a genuine
respect and love for Peter. They are not words I use lightly. When I
resigned from the Hamlyn Group to set out on my own, he was
quick to arrange a meeting with me at the Hyatt Hotel in Sydney.
His greeting, as best as I can recall, was "Weldon, you bastard,
whatever you're up to I want part of the action!" It was a
wonderful gesture of faith from a powerful friend. Let's face it,
even the high-profile head of a very successful group can soon be
forgotten once he or she has left. But Peter wasn't given to such
lapses of memory.

I told him I held a strong belief that we should publish the first
Australian language dictionary, but I needed convincing that
Queensland's Jacaranda Press and Macquarie University had all the
material at hand. I wanted to spend $20 000 checking the

university's comprehensive reference system — all set down on cards — and then invest more in stages.

"If you're serious," I said, "just put $10 000 in my bank account on Monday and you've got a third of the business."

First thing Monday the cheque arrived and, together with my own money, we were under way. (Four years later his $10 000 investment was worth $650 000!) Lyn Holloway of Straits Times Press was another friend to assist in the publication of Australia's first authoritative language dictionary, *The Macquarie Dictionary*. To this day their contributions are acknowledged in the publication, particularly Peter's.

Peter got out of the newspaper business way before his time. Why? Because he had the guts to keep his word. Without going into details, he must have been bitterly disappointed by some of the small-minded people around him he thought he could depend upon.

To me, Peter stood tall as one of the brightest new people in the newspaper industry in his time — a visionary who insisted on getting the facts absolutely right. He is also a compassionate man who knows when to relax and have fun.

I recall being Peter's guest at the opening of one of his friend's restaurants in Adelaide. Towards the end of the evening I rose from our crowded table and pretended to pull the tablecloth off with everything still on the table. Peter, as was his style, immediately challenged me to do it and put his money down. When I hesitated Peter called the restaurateur and promised to cover any breakages. The whole restaurant stood back while I did my act. I grabbed the cloth like one of the world's great matadors, albeit one imbued with Dutch courage rather than the real thing. Bracing for the shower of crockery and cutlery, I whipped the cloth off. Every single item still stood on the bare table! Peter was absolutely astonished, but no-one was more surprised than me!

In the years that followed, I created a worldwide fraternity based around the tablecloth-pulling-in-a-crowded-restaurant trick. Though *usually* successful, it has cost the company reparations from time to time. For that I can thank Peter, the author of that original challenge in Adelaide.

He is still lazing about in retirement, God bless him.

# Philip Jarvis

*Books can be sold like soap!*

Philip Jarvis was the chief buyer for Boots chemists in England when he met Paul Hamlyn. Paul invited Philip to leave Boots to be his managing director, and it was Philip who persuaded Paul to use his own name for the publishing of new books a year later. It was clear to Philip that what Paul needed was a publisher, not a managing director, so Philip took over the editorial, production and design. Together they became great friends and a magic business combination.

It was Philip who coined some of the memorable marketing quotes that have become part of industry legend, such as "Books can be sold like soap!" This very stylish fellow was, I believe, the man most responsible for giving Paul Hamlyn books their unique "buy-me" look. He certainly inspired me to be stylish in publishing and to extend every effort to get the best packaging.

# Rupert Murdoch

*... his success as an Australian overseas*
*continually inspired me.*

I first heard of Rupert Murdoch when I was a junior branch manager at Grenville's. From memory, he had just taken the reins of a relatively small Adelaide newspaper, *The News*, at the age of twenty-three. It was a legacy from his legendary father, Sir Keith Murdoch, who had directed the hugely successful Herald & Weekly Times newspaper conglomerate in Melbourne.

Rupert Murdoch was so obviously the youngest figure in the publishing world of the 1960s that it was probably natural for me to lionise him. I followed his every move on the path to success. I was able to predict every occasion his opposition in the newspaper establishment would underestimate him. With each success the same establishment would console itself with the thought that this energetic young upstart would slip up next time and finally go bust. (The establishment said exactly the same about me during my career path because I was young, energetic and outspoken.)

When Fairfax and Packer sold Rupert Murdoch *The Mirror* afternoon newspaper in Sydney, they were convinced it would be the straw to break the camel's back. The rest is history.

I first met Rupert Murdoch when he came to the official launch of the Paul Hamlyn Group in 1968. To Paul's great surprise he didn't arrive for a few drinks and leave early. He was a typical Australian executive in that he circulated and spoke with everyone. He certainly paid me a great compliment just by being there.

I had several cordial meetings with him over the years, and when I decided to embark on publishing in America we formed a joint venture to produce a book — *A Salute to Texas* — commemorating 150 years of statehood. Driven by Murdoch's San Antonio-based paper, *The Express News* (the first newspaper he acquired in the US), the book was promoted through newspapers state-wide. One of our customers, Bill Marbett, ran the regional newspaper group which had sold Murdoch *The Express News*. He told me, "That Aussie friend of yours has amazed us. When we had the *The Express News* it was losing millions a year. So when Murdoch made an offer out of the blue we thought we'd made a killing. We thought this guy couldn't hope to reverse the paper's fortunes if we couldn't, yet it now makes $17 million a year." Marbett hadn't realised that Murdoch, very much a hands-on person, knew every aspect of the newspaper industry.

His success as an Australian overseas continually inspired me. I remember when he first went to England. The Hamlyn Group was a subsidiary of IPC at the time and IPC owned the biggest daily newspaper in England, the London *Daily Mirror*. IPC also had *The Sun*, founded as a left wing union newspaper. It had a circulation of 750 000 and was losing a lot of money when Murdoch bought it for £250 000.

Soon after, I was dining in Soho with IPC board members Hugh Cudlip, Gordon Cartwright, Ellis Bourke and Paul Hamlyn. When I asked Cudlip how he thought Murdoch would go in England, my question was ignored. After some pressing, he pronounced, "It's one thing to run a small newspaper in Australia, but Murdoch will soon discover he is dealing with the Fleet Street boys here."

Here we go again, I thought. They are going to give him a head start by underestimating him, and by the time they wake up it will be too late. I recall a marvellously clever one-liner by one of his top circulation people: "*The Mirror* will reach four million copies before we do with *The Sun!*" The *Mirror* circulation at that time was over five million and *The Sun*'s a paltry 250 000.

Sure enough, it wasn't that long before *The Sun* climbed to a four million circulation. Murdoch had done it again.

Alec Mackay, the director in charge of marketing at IPC, was a brilliant Australian. He knew every trick there was about getting advertising revenue. When Alec was retired early from IPC on medical grounds (after some political falling-out), Murdoch snapped him up for News Limited. It was no coincidence. When Murdoch entered a new market, he would often pick up an experienced industry adviser, occasionally someone who had just retired. This enabled him to get a quick grasp on the key issues and then add his own energetic vision. He certainly achieved this with Alec Mackay.

He also brought in some of his brightest promotion and circulation people from Australia. And since many Australian business people nurse a keen desire to prove we can succeed in any English-speaking country, those Murdoch drafted were fiercely determined.

I have never encountered a business person with more courage, patience and perseverance than Rupert Murdoch. He launched *The Australian* newspaper with a vision to create the country's first national daily newspaper. It was regarded as an impossible objective because of the country's distant, isolated and relatively small population centres, all served by entrenched local newspapers. Murdoch hung in despite large losses for many, many years (as he did with *The Mirror)*. Critics rarely give him marks for overall performance, yet he has saved more jobs in the publishing industry than anyone else. Had it not been for Murdoch, newspapers like *The Mirror* and *The Express News* and *The Times* would have closed, throwing thousands out of work.

Murdoch's perseverance since the crash of 1987 has been remarkable. When the whole world economy crashed it left him exposed through some of his major acquisitions and visionary projects, such as Sky Television. Yet he has rebounded superbly and there's no doubt in my mind that Sky Television, for one, will eventually be an enormous cash cow. I'm just as sure that ultimately he will be rewarded for his perseverance with television in America.

Murdoch is the quintessential business success, single-handedly picking up loss-making entities over many years and transforming them into solid operations. Through the most testing economic climates one could imagine, he has continued to lead the media industry around the world. Though now an American citizen, he's living proof that a boy from Adelaide can become a hugely successful global publisher. He is certainly an inspiration to me, just as he should be to every young person in business. Murdoch's example confirms that you can't do it without hard work or taking risks.

Over the years, no matter how elevated his profile, I've always been able to telephone him or have a meeting. I have a shareholding in a company in America with one of his subsidiaries and I'm proud of that relationship. He has done me small favours that he wouldn't even remember. And a few years back he made a statement I regard as the ultimate compliment: "Kevin, you and I are of similar spirit."

# Ralph Vernon-Hunt

*He also taught me to never be hoodwinked*
*by the so-called specialists ...*

Paul Hamlyn enticed this truly unique sales director away from Pan
Books, where he enjoyed the reputation of a guy loved by everyone.
Certainly customers loved him. They couldn't help giving him
orders. For his part, he treated most customers as genuinely close
friends. Suffice to say that he was one of the few Englishmen in a
top position who got on really well with the rough Aussies in
Australian publishing and bookselling.

For instance, the Forsyth brothers, owners of the large book outlet
Dymocks, were severe on staff and invariably exacted their pound of
flesh. Yet they always looked forward to Ralph's visits and he would
leave the country with huge orders. He had the ability to bring good
humour into his business dealings and was a superbly witty after-
dinner speaker. He was equally amusing on company politics!

I remember a time in England when IPC called in the divisional
managers of their subsidiaries because some specialist — a
pontifical and humourless soul — had decided to convert all
offices to open plan. Though he clearly cared little for dissenting
opinion, he lightly asked if there were any questions.

In came Ralph. "Why don't I think the manager's office should
be open plan? My immediate staff would be able to tell you more
vividly, were they not so shy, so I'll tell you for them. Like
everybody else in private, I pick my nose. Even worse, I lift my left
cheek occasionally to, well, fart. And rumour has it that I've been
known to be even more outrageous in the office. Thus, dear man,
*my* office will not be in any open plan.

"When I told one of your idiots to bugger off out of my office, he
claimed that he *had* to measure whether I was a two-window or one-
window office to decide whether it could be converted! Why on
earth are you wasting the shareholders' money with such absurdity?"

The meeting disintegrated as Ralph made his exit.

I recall another telling remark Ralph made while we were having
dinner in Australia with an awfully snobbish Englishman, who led

an American publishing company. After asking for my views on the Australian publishing scene, he promptly interrupted to lecture me about my home territory. *Why had he bothered to ask me in the first place*, I wondered, at which point Ralph leaned across and whispered, "Kevin, this is just the sort of Pom who gives good Poms a bad name in Australia."

Ralph taught me to make firm friends in business, to enjoy their company and to crack a joke now and then. He also taught me never to be hoodwinked by the so-called specialists if you have practical reasons to oppose bureaucratic advice.

Ralph sadly died of emphysema several years ago, though we still see his wonderful wife when we visit England.

# Sam Johnson

*Sam Johnson had a big influence on my career by exposing me to his methods of management ...*

Sam Johnson is one of the wealthiest men in the USA. His family owns the Johnson Wax Company, established in over fifty countries.

I first met Sam through a mutual interest in seaplane flying. Sam has flown seaplanes for most of his life, flying off into the wilds of Canada and Alaska to camp and fish. I published a small seaplane club magazine in Australia at the time and Sam and I corresponded when he decided to buy a twin-engine Australian-built Nomad to put on floats. It was a brilliant success, as it turned out.

He invited me to visit him in Racine, Wisconsin, while I was visiting the USA in 1982. It was at this point that Sam Johnson had a big influence on my career by exposing me to his methods of management. These included his approach to the environment, his paternalism, his goodwill, his treatment of present and past staff, and his humility.

The Johnson Wax Company introduced a profit-sharing scheme in 1928, which has continued ever since. They have had a mission statement since then too, upon which I have based my own company's mission statement. They have holiday apartments around the world for staff use and charitable trusts to help needy causes.

The Johnson head office in Racine is a classic heritage trust building which, along with all the office furniture, was designed by Frank Lloyd Wright. (The home Sam was raised in was also designed by Lloyd Wright. It has been turned over to charitable institutions these days.)

The Johnson guesthouse, where I stayed, was built expressly to house visitors. To decorate the guesthouse and its grounds, Sam sent his sister around the world to buy art and sculpture from every country in which they had a business. Everything is of such stylish excellence that it has become a unique collection in its own right.

But what left the most indelible impression was that the 75-year-old man who picked me up from the station and drove me around had retired from Johnson Wax ten years earlier. Sam offers a lot of his retirees work if they need it. I thought this was a wonderful attitude and have adopted it for my own company ever since. It gives the company some soul.

# Simon Simpson

*Simon taught me that you must take time out*
*of your busy life to look after yourself.*

The founding managing director of La Roche pharmaceutical company in Australia, Simon Simpson, built a magnificent office and factory complex in Dee Why, with striking architecture and beautifully landscaped gardens. He also built a cosmetic company in the middle of a beautiful adjoining forest. His example inspired me when I built the Hamlyn complex, making me determined to build a beautiful working environment in which the local community could take pride.

Simon was marvellously casual and seemed to lead with a minimum of fuss. He had a yacht designed much like a Thames barge with a drop keel. Its flat bottom enabled it to be carried on the deck of cargo vessels and shipped to any area he fancied. When it arrived at its destination, he'd get it victualled and rigged and would then sail for three months around some of the most exotic waterways in the world.

When Simon, a divorcee, met a young woman who said she'd like to crew for him, he told her she would have to be highly-skilled in astro-navigation. He didn't really want to take her. Unperturbed, she mastered the skill and earned a spot on his yacht. She would travel on the cargo vessel with the yacht to the destination required, taking practice sights along the way. Simon and his crew member subsequently married. He passed away some years ago.

Simon taught me that you must take some time out of your busy life to look after yourself. "Will people remember whether you took time off from a busy schedule to enjoy yourself if the profits are booming?" he would ask rhetorically.

# Leslie Weldon, my uncle

*This man is surely a big business tycoon, I thought,*
*and if one Weldon can do it, maybe I can, too, some day.*

My grandfather's brother was a great inspiration to me in business. As a young boy I spent holidays in Sydney with him. Here was a relative with a big house at Pymble that I loved, a huge Buick car and a big panelled office in the centre of the city, replete with buttons and switches. Just like the movies. This man is surely a big business tycoon, I thought, and if one Weldon can do it, maybe I can, too, some day.

Uncle Leslie founded Manufacturers Mutual Insurance (MMI) with £1000. He told me that he had no back-up or underwriting business when he started, so he wrote to every large insurance company in England. He said (in part): "I'm Leslie Weldon and, having just founded an Australian insurance company, I obviously haven't much to offer you other than vision, energy and hard work." He succeeded with the relatively few who replied. By the time he retired, MMI was one of the most successful insurance companies in the country.

I did much the same when I started the Hamlyn Group. I cheekily wrote to every newspaper and magazine publisher in Australia, explaining that I was starting the Hamlyn Group and would like the right to use material from their archives. All refused except the Fairfax Group. Rupert Henderson wrote to suggest I meet Tom Farrell, the chief editorial director who was also responsible for their magazine subsidiary, Sungravure. The first result of that cheeky letter was the re-use of material from the *Woman's Day* magazine. Called *The Margaret Fulton Cookbook*, it went on to sell 1.5 million copies. I learned a good thing from Uncle Leslie!